LUXURY GARDENS

UK & IRELAND

edited by Elke Fleing

teNeues

Poolewe

Banchory

Falkland

Trentham
Northwich
Chirk
Welshpool
Tal-y-Cafn
Portmeirion

Moreton-in-Marsh
Devauden

Great Torrington

Adare

Bantry

Colchester
Ockley   Sissinghurst
Woking
Fontwell
East Cowes

Southampton
Romsey
Stourton
Falmouth
St. Austell
Barrington
Bodmin
Cheddon Fitzpaine
Buckfastleigh
Marldon

Luxury Gardens

UK & IRELAND

The Beauty of Sculptured Nature

Around the world, garden design is an ancient tradition dating back for centuries. As for any artistic expression, the designs also mirror contemporary life, social developments and prevailing worldviews.

In medieval times, in the western world the idea of nature's beauty, once popular in antiquity, had all but vanished: gardens emerged as fruit and vegetable plots or pleasure gardens which were cordoned off from nature's wilderness. The rediscovery of a pastoral lifestyle during the Italian Renaissance led to a resurgence of the garden's importance. The legacy of antiquity was revived, and villa gardens were distinguished by perfect harmony between the house and an artfully designed garden. Terraces, staircases, geometric parterres with hedge-lined arcades, avenues and a rich store of sculptures and fountains were the main features. Vistas were staged and in the mid-16th century, parterres frequently created a majestic atmosphere and were designed for representation.

Even if elements of Baroque garden design were already evident in Italy, this style triumphed in France. Evolving in the 17th century from the Renaissance garden, its characteristic feature was an axial line in relation to the main house and greater symmetry of the expansive parterres. The age of Absolutism and the idea of nature as something to be subdued and domesticated favoured this design principle that was expressed in strict topiaries and geometric parterres.

In Great Britain and Ireland, garden design was initially a reaction to developments in other countries. Design features of Italian Renaissance gardens were initially blended with medieval forms. After 1600, the Italian influence was even greater. By the end of the Civil War and the return of Charles II from French exile in 1660, the principles of French Baroque parterres emerged in English garden design, albeit with a unique approach. The axial line of French gardens never triumphed in England, and from 1690, this feature was even more heavily repressed, with parterres not always created in strict symmetry as well as a lack of closed forms and visible boundaries across the parterres.

From the first half of the 18th century, a radical change gradually emerged in previous perceptions of space and nature. As a result of upheaval in agriculture and a rejection of the Absolutist order, landscape gardens emerged at the country residences of liberal aristocrats. Geometric composition principles were relaxed, topiaries were relinquished and landscape views opened up. Landscapes were to be created in imitation of nature. The endeavour was to connect nature, poetry and painting in a unified form. In the mid-18th century, English gardens increasingly resembled an ideal Arcadian landscape with park architectures that created manifold rooms with picturesque vistas. The key inspirations were from East-Asian garden design with its love of nature and the "art of irregularity". The distinction between garden and free landscape was increasingly blurred. From 1750, under Lancelot "Capability" Brown, the manifold forms in the gardens were reduced to a few, eye-catching features. Extensive lawns, reflecting lakes and tree groups dominated the simple beauty of landscape. In the late 18th century, the popular demand was for genuine romantic wilderness with rapid-flowing streams and ruins. During this period, flowerbeds and perennials still retained their popularity, with new exotic plant collections being introduced for variation, which was absent in the parkland.

The 19th century revealed a multiplicity of less linear styles. Past designs were rediscovered, reworked, combined and new, exotic plants and tree collections changed the gardens' appearance. Garden design journals provided information on plants and modern growing methods and glasshouses and rockeries complemented the picture. The Italianate style with terrace, ornamental garden and sophisticated parterres was also included as well as French-inspired gravel parterres with box hedges or old English gardens with topiaries, simple floral collections and herb gardens. The common feature of all these styles was that they were an anti-thesis to the idyllic 18th century landscape garden. Not until 1870, did a new trend emerge that was in touch with nature. Designs with plants and colour groupings emerged, charming, natural "wild country garden estates" became fashionable and won key advocates in the garden designers William Robinson and Gertrude Jekyll. Their ideas influenced garden design almost throughout the 20th century, yet always leaving space for modern approaches and new interpretations.

Elke Fleing

Die Schönheit gelenkter Natur

Gartenkunst hat weltweit eine jahrtausendealte Tradition und wie jeder künstlerische Ausdruck ist auch sie ein Spiegel der jeweiligen Zeit und ihrer gesellschaftlichen Entwicklungen und vorherrschenden Weltanschauungen.

Während im abendländischen Mittelalter die Vorstellung von der Schönheit der Natur, wie sie die Antike noch kannte, verschwunden war und Gärten als abgegrenzte Nutz- oder Lustgärten gegenüber der Wildnis in Erscheinung traten, erfuhr der Garten in der italienischen Renaissance eine Aufwertung durch die Wiederentdeckung des Landlebens. Das antike Erbe lebte auf und die Villengärten zeichneten sich durch eine große Harmonie zwischen Haus und künstlerisch durchgeformtem Garten aus. Terrassen, Treppen, geometrische, von Hecken gerahmte Beete, Laubengänge, Alleen und eine reiche Ausstattung mit Skulpturen und Brunnen waren seine Hauptmerkmale. Ausblicke wurden inszeniert und Mitte des 16. Jahrhunderts dienten die Anlagen nicht selten der Prachtentfaltung und Repräsentation.

Auch wenn sich Elemente barocker Gartengestaltung schon in Italien finden lassen, erreichte diese in Frankreich ihren Höhepunkt. Sie entwickelte sich im 17. Jahrhundert aus dem Renaissancegarten und wurde durch die axiale Ausrichtung des Gartens auf das Hauptgebäude, größere Symmetrie und Ausbreitung in der Fläche geprägt. Der Absolutismus und die Vorstellung von der Natur als etwas zu Unterwerfendes und zu Domestizierendes begünstigte dieses Gestaltungsprinzip, was seinen Ausdruck im strengen Formschnitt der Pflanzen (Topiaria) und der Anlage von Parterres in geometrischen Mustern fand.

In Großbritannien und Irland hat sich die Gartenkunst zunächst als Reaktion auf die Entwicklung in anderen Ländern herausgebildet. Die Gestaltungselemente italienischer Renaissancegärten wurden zunächst mit solchen des Mittelalters gemischt. Nach 1600 wurde der italienische Einfluss dann stärker. Mit dem Ende des Bürgerkrieges und der Rückkehr Karls II. aus dem französischen Exil 1660 fanden die Prinzipien französischer Barockanlagen Eingang in die englische Gartengestaltung, die in ihrer Konzeption jedoch auch jetzt eigenständig blieb. Die axiale Ausrichtung französischer Gärten triumphierte in England nie und wurde ab 1690 noch stärker zurückgedrängt, die Anlage erfolgte nicht immer in strenger Symmetrie, es fehlte die Geschlossenheit und eine sichtbare Grenze der Gesamtanlage.

Ab der ersten Hälfte des 18. Jahrhunderts vollzog sich in England ein langsamer, aber radikaler Wandel der bisherigen Wahrnehmung von Raum und Natur. Infolge eines Umbruchs in der Landwirtschaft und als Absage an die absolutistische Ordo-Vorstellung entwickelte sich der Landschaftsgarten auf den Landsitzen liberaler Adeliger. Geometrische Kompositionsprinzipien wurden gelockert, ungeschnittene Bäume verwendet, der Blick in die Landschaft geöffnet. Eine der Natur nachempfundene Landschaft sollte geschaffen werden, indem man versuchte, die Natur, Poesie und Malerei zu einer Einheit zu verbinden. Mitte des 18. Jahrhunderts glichen englische Gärten immer mehr einer idealen arkadischen Landschaft mit Parkarchitekturen, die vielfältige Räume mit pittoresken Bildern schufen. Wichtige Impulse kamen dabei von der ostasiatischen Gartenkunst mit ihrer Liebe zur Natur und ihrer „Kunst der Unregelmäßigkeit". Die Grenze zwischen Garten und freier Landschaft verwischte zunehmend. Unter Lancelot „Capability" Brown wurden ab 1750 die vielfältigen Formen in den Gärten auf wenige markante Erscheinungen reduziert. Weite Grasflächen, spiegelnde Seen und Baumgruppen beherrschten die schlichte Schönheit der Landschaft. Ende des 18. Jahrhunderts forderte man dann echte romantische Wildheit mit reißenden Bächen und Ruinen. Während dieser ganzen Zeit hatten Blumen- und Strauchgärten, bestückt mit neuen, exotischen Pflanzen, jedoch Bestand und lieferten die Abwechslung, die der Park vermissen ließ.

Das 19. Jahrhundert war vielgesichtig, weniger gradlinig in der Entwicklung. Vergangene Moden wurden erneut aufgegriffen, umgearbeitet, kombiniert und neue, exotische Pflanzen und Bäume veränderten das Aussehen der Gärten. Gartenjournale informierten über Pflanzen und moderne Zuchttechniken, Gewächshäuser und Steingärten ergänzten das Bild. Der italienische Stil mit Terrasse, Ziergarten und raffinierten Beetanlagen gehörte genauso dazu wie französisch inspirierte Kiesparterres mit Buchsbaumeinfassungen oder altenglische Gärten mit Formbäumen, schlichten Blumen und Kräutergarten. Allen Stilen war gemeinsam, dass sie eine Antithese zur idyllischen Landschaft des 18. Jahrhunderts bildeten. Erst ab 1870 zeichnet sich eine neue Tendenz zur Naturnähe ab. Die Gestaltung mit Pflanzen- und Farbgruppen kam auf, reizvolle, natürliche „Bauerngärten" kamen in Mode und diese fand in William Robinson und Gertrude Jekyll bedeutende Vertreter. Ihre Vorstellungen prägten die Gartenkunst fast während des ganzen 20. Jahrhunderts, ließen aber stets Raum für moderne Ansätze und Neuinterpretationen.

Elke Fleing

La beauté d'une nature modelée

De par le monde, l'architecture du paysage est une tradition millénaire et comme toute forme d'expression artistique, elle est aussi le reflet d'une époque, de son évolution sociale et de sa conception prévalente du monde.

Tandis que dans l'occident du Moyen-Âge la perception de la beauté de la nature, telle que l'Antiquité la connaissait, avait disparu et que les jardins étaient devenus des potagers utilitaires ou des jardins des plaisir fermés, par opposition à la nature sauvage, la Renaissance italienne réinventa le jardin en redécouvrant la vie à la campagne. L'héritage de l'Antiquité se raviva et les jardins des villas se distinguaient par la parfaite harmonie entre l'habitation et le jardin ordonné artistiquement. Terrasses, escaliers, parterres géométriques, bordés de haies, tonnelles, allées, décors fastueux de statues et de jets d'eau en constituaient les caractéristiques principales. Les perspectives étaient mises en scène et au milieu du 16ème siècle, les parcs servaient souvent à représenter et à déployer faste et puissance.

Même s'il y a en Italie quelques éléments de la conception baroque du jardin, c'est en France que celle-ci atteignit son apogée. Issue du style de la Renaissance, elle se développa au 17ème siècle. Elle était marquée par l'alignement du jardin dans l'axe du bâtiment principal, une plus grande symétrie et l'extension des surfaces. L'absolutisme et l'idée d'une nature à dompter et à domestiquer sous-tendaient ses principes de conception qui reposaient sur l'abondance des topiaires (arbustes taillés rigoureusement comme des sculptures) et les parterres de broderie géométriques.

En Grande-Bretagne et en Irlande, l'architecture du paysage émergea en réaction aux évolutions dans les autres pays. Les éléments de composition des jardins de la Renaissance italienne furent tout d'abord mêlés à ceux du Moyen-Âge. Après 1600, l'influence italienne se renforça. A la fin de la guerre civile et au retour de Charles II de son exil français en 1660, les principes des jardins baroques français firent leur apparition dans l'élaboration des jardins anglais dont la conception demeura toutefois indépendante. L'axialisation du jardin à la française n'ayant jamais triomphé en Angleterre, elle sera encore davantage écartée à partir de 1690. La stricte symétrie n'était pas toujours respectée, il manquait l'unité de composition et une délimitation visible de l'ensemble du parc.

À l'aube du 18ème siècle s'opéra en Angleterre une mutation lente mais radicale de la perception de l'espace et de la nature. À la suite de profonds changements dans l'agriculture et par refus de la conception absolutiste de l'Ordo le jardin paysager se développa sur les terres des aristocrates. Les principes de composition géométrique s'assouplirent, les arbres ne furent pas taillés, la vue s'ouvrit sur le paysage environnant. Le style du jardin paysager redécouvre la nature sous son aspect sauvage et poétique à travers la peinture. Au milieu du 18ème siècle, dans ses divers tableaux, le jardin à l'anglaise formait des compositions pittoresques et ressemblait de plus en plus aux paysages de l'idyllique Arcadie. De ses diverses sources d'inspiration, la plus importante fut celle du jardin extrême-oriental, avec son goût pour la nature et pour l'irrégularité de la composition. La différence entre jardin et nature libre s'estompa de plus en plus. À partir de 1750, avec le paysagiste Lancelot Brown, plus connu sous le nom de Capability Brown, on préféra à la diversité des formes quelques effets marquants : l'ondulation de vastes étendues herbeuses, le reflet des pièces d'eau, les rideaux d'arbres soulignaient la simple beauté du paysage. La fin du 18ème siècle connut un engouement par un romantisme ostensible avec des ruines et des ruisseaux impétueux. Simultanément, l'intérêt se porta également vers les jardins de fleurs et d'arbustes agrémentés de nouvelles plantes exotiques, qui abondaient alors d'une flore diversifiée.

Le 19ème siècle connut des mutations esthétiques et fut moins rectiligne dans son évolution. On reprit, transforma et déclina des modes passées. De nouvelles essences exotiques de plantes et d'arbres modifièrent l'apparence des jardins. Des revues de jardinage commencèrent à fournir des informations sur les plantes et les méthodes de culture. Serres et jardins de rocaille complétaient le tableau. C'est la diversité des styles: style italien avec ses terrasses, jardin d'agrément et plates-bandes raffinées mais aussi parterres de gravier à la française entourés de massifs de buis ou vieux jardins anglais avec des topiaires, de simples fleurs et des jardins d'herbes aromatiques. Tous ces styles représentaient l'antithèse du paysage idyllique du 18ème siècle. À partir de 1870 on eut tendance à se rapprocher de la nature. La vogue des jardins de campagne naturels et agréables apparut et des personnalités comme William Robinson et Gertrude Jekyll introduisirent la composition par groupes de plantes et de couleurs. Leurs créations marquèrent l'architecture du paysage pendant presque tout le 20ème siècle, tout en laissant le champ libre à des approches modernes et des interprétations innovantes.

Elke Fleing

La belleza de la naturaleza matizada por el hombre

El arte de la jardinería goza de una tradición milenaria en todo el mundo y, como es propio de toda expresión artística, también es reflejo de su época y de los desarrollos sociales y modos de ver la vida predominantes en su momento.

Mientras que a finales de la Edad Media occidental el concepto de la belleza natural había desaparecido tal y como se conocía en la antigüedad y los jardines destacaban como jardines útiles o de recreo frente a la naturaleza salvaje, en el renacimiento italiano la jardinería experimentó una revalorización gracias al redescubrimiento de la vida campestre. Así, florecieron las antiguas herencias, y los jardines de villas empezaron a caracterizarse por una gran armonía entre edificios y jardines formales. Las terrazas, escaleras, arrietes geométricos enmarcados por setos, alamedas de hojarasca, avenidas y una rica presencia de esculturas y fuentes eran sus principales características. Se modelaban vistas panorámicas y, a mediados del siglo XVI, los parques y jardines a menudo servían para desplegar la suntuosidad y la representatividad de sus propietarios.

Si bien en Italia ya encontramos elementos barrocos de diseño de jardines, éstos experimentan su momento álgido en Francia. Se desarrollaron en el siglo XVII de los jardines renacentistas y, gracias a la orientación axial del jardín, proporcionaban una mayor simetría y extensión al edificio principal. El absolutismo y la concepción de la naturaleza como algo supeditable y domesticable favoreció este principio de diseño, algo que también se expresaba en los cortes estrictos de las plantas (topiaria) y la creación de parterres con dibujos geométricos.

En Gran Bretaña e Irlanda, la jardinería primero surgió como reacción al desarrollo experimentado en otros países. Al principio, los elementos decorativos de los jardines renacentistas italianos se entremezclaron con los medievales. Tras el año 1600, la influencia italiana se fortaleció. Con el fin de la guerra civil y la vuelta de Carlos II. de su exilio en Francia en 1660, los jardines barrocos galos comenzaron a aplicarse en el paisajismo inglés, cuya concepción sin embargo continuó siendo independiente. La orientación axial de los jardines franceses nunca triunfó en Inglaterra, y a partir de 1690 aún fue refrenada con mayor ahínco; los jardines no siempre presentaban una simetría estricta, faltaba la armonía de conjunto y un cierre visual del jardín en su conjunto.

Desde la primera mitad del siglo XVIII, en Inglaterra se vivió un cambio lento pero radical de la percepción del espacio y la naturaleza existente hasta el momento. Como consecuencia de una revolución en la agricultura y como negativa a todo pensamiento de orden absolutista, el paisajismo se desarrolló en las propiedades de la nobleza liberal. Se aligeraron los principios de composición geométrica, se utilizaron árboles no recortados y se abrió la vista hacia el paisaje. Se pretendía crear paisajes compenetrados con la naturaleza intentando fraguar una unidad entre naturaleza, poesía y pintura. A mediados del siglo XVIII los jardines ingleses se parecían cada vez más a un paisaje arcádico ideal con arquitectura paisajística, que creaban espacios variados con imágenes pintorescas. El arte paisajístico del lejano oriente daba impulsos importantes con su amor por la naturaleza y su "arte de la irregularidad". La frontera entre el jardín y el paisaje silvestre se iba difuminando cada vez más. Con Lancelot "Capability" Brown, a partir de 1750 las formas variadas de los jardines fueron reduciéndose a unas pocas visiones destacadas. Los amplios céspedes, lagos reflectantes y agrupaciones de árboles dominaban la llana belleza del paisaje. A finales del siglo XVIII se comenzó a fomentar el aire silvestre y romántico, con raudos arroyos y ruinas. Sin embargo, durante todo este tiempo, los jardines de flores y arbustos dotados de nuevas plantas exóticas continuaron existiendo, y proporcionaban la diversidad extrañada en los parques.

El siglo XIX fue polifacético, con una línea de desarrollo mucho más difusa. Las antiguas modas volvieron a retomarse, trabajarse y combinarse, y nuevos árboles y plantas exóticas modificaron el aspecto de los jardines. Las revistas sobre jardinería informaban sobre las plantas y las técnicas modernas de cultivo, y los invernaderos y los jardines rocosos complementaban el panorama. El estilo italiano, con terraza, jardín de recreo y refinados arriates estaba tan presente como las parcelas de gravilla de inspiración francesa, con bordes de arbusto o jardines ingleses antiguos con árboles moldeados, flores sencillas y jardines de hierbas. Todos los estilos tenían en común que formaban una antítesis al idílico paisaje del siglo XVIII. A partir de 1870 empezó a perfilarse una nueva tendencia hacia la naturaleza silvestre. La creación con grupos de plantas y grupos cromáticos prosperó, poniendo de moda interesantes "huertas de ocio" naturales, que encontraron importantes representantes con William Robinson y Gertrude Jekyll. Sus ideas caracterizaron el arte paisajístico prácticamente durante todo el siglo XX, dejando siempre espacio para enfoques modernos y nuevas interpretaciones.

Elke Fleing

La bellezza della natura domata

L'arte del giardinaggio ha in tutto il mondo una tradizione millenaria. Come ogni espressione artistica, essa rispecchia gli sviluppi sociali e la concezione del mondo tipici del proprio tempo.

Mentre nel Medioevo occidentale era venuta meno la concezione della bellezza della natura propria dell'antichità ed erano comparsi orti e giardini delle delizie come spazi chiusi in contrapposizione alla natura selvaggia, nel Rinascimento italiano si assiste ad una rivalutazione del giardino dovuta alla riscoperta della vita rurale. Un patrimonio ancestrale tornò a nuova vita: i parchi che circondavano le ville erano caratterizzati dalla perfetta armonia tra la casa e il giardino curato ad arte, i cui elementi principali erano terrazze, scalinate, aiuole geometriche orlate di siepi, arcate, viali ed un'infinità di sculture e di fontane. Da più punti si poteva godere il panorama: a metà del XVI secolo i parchi avevano non raramente funzione di rappresentazione e di mera esibizione di sfarzo.

Anche se già in Italia l'arte dell'allestimento dei giardini rivelava elementi barocchi, fu in Francia che essi raggiunsero il culmine. Tale concezione si evolse nel corso del XVII secolo prendendo spunto dal giardino rinascimentale ed era caratterizzata dalla direzione assiale del parco rispetto all'edificio principale, da una maggiore simmetria e dall'estensione della superficie. L'assolutismo e l'idea della natura come qualcosa da sottomettere e da domare favorirono tale canone di allestimento, che trovò espressione nella potatura severa delle piante (arte topiaria) e nella realizzazione di parterre a disegni geometrici.

In Gran Bretagna e in Irlanda il giardinaggio artistico ha avuto origine, in primo luogo, come reazione allo sviluppo in altri paesi. Gli elementi propri dei giardini rinascimentali italiani vennero dapprima fusi con quelli medioevali. Dopo il 1600 l'influsso italiano si accentuò. Con la fine della guerra civile e il ritorno di Carlo II dall'esilio, i canoni dei parchi barocchi francesi entrarono a far parte dell'allestimento inglese, che continuò tuttavia a godere di una propria autonomia. La direzione assiale dei giardini francesi non si affermò mai in Inghilterra e cadde sempre più in disuso dopo il 1690: non sempre la simmetria era rigorosa, e mancavano l'unità ed un limite visibile del parco.

In Inghilterra, a partire dalla prima metà del XVIII secolo, la percezione dello spazio e della natura iniziò a trasformarsi lentamente ma in modo radicale. In seguito al profondo cambiamento in atto nell'agricoltura e come espressione di rifiuto dell'idea assolutistica della divisione in classi, il giardino all'inglese si affermò presso la nobiltà liberale. I principi compositivi geometrici vennero attenuati e si passò all'utilizzo di alberi non potati, aprendo la vista al paesaggio. L'obiettivo era creare uno scenario a imitazione del creato con l'intento di ridurre ad un unico insieme natura, poesia e pittura. A metà del XVIII secolo i giardini inglesi assunsero sempre più l'aspetto di ideali paesaggi arcadici con architetture in cui molteplici spazi schiudevano scorci pittoreschi. In tale contesto, il giardinaggio artistico dell'estremo Oriente, imperniato sull'amore per la natura e sull'"arte dell'irregolarità", fornì impulsi significativi. La linea di demarcazione tra giardino e paesaggio si fece sempre meno netta. Con Lancelot "Capability" Brown, a partire dal 1750, le molteplici forme assunte dai giardini si ridussero a pochi esempi degni di nota. Vaste superfici erbose, specchi d'acqua e gruppi arborei dominavano la semplice bellezza del paesaggio. Alla fine del XVIII secolo il gusto si orientò verso una natura selvaggia tipicamente romantica, con torrenti in piena e rocce in rovina. Durante tutto questo tempo continuarono tuttavia a esistere giardini di fiori e di arbusti arricchiti da piante nuove ed esotiche, in cui si trovava quella varietà che mancava ai parchi.

Il XIX secolo rivelò molti aspetti meno lineari nel loro sviluppo. Si rivisitarono le mode passate, mentre piante e alberi esotici modificarono l'aspetto dei giardini. Le riviste di giardinaggio fornivano informazioni su piante e su moderne tecniche di coltivazione, serre e giardini alla giapponese diedero il tocco finale. Lo stile italiano con terrazze, giardinetti e aiuole accattivanti continuò a sussistere accanto ai parterre di ghiaia francesi circondati da bossi, o ai giardini di gusto "Old England" con alberi potati ad arte, fiori comuni e orticelli. Tutti questi stili avevano in comune l'antitesi che esprimevano nei confronti del paesaggio idilliaco del XVIII secolo. Solo dopo il 1870 si delineò una nuova tendenza che si riavvicinava alla natura. Fu la volta dei gruppi di piante e di colori, deliziosi orti naturali divennero "en vogue"; William Robinson e Gertrude Jekyll furono i rappresentanti di questa tendenza. Le loro idee influenzarono il giardinaggio artistico per quasi tutto il XX secolo, lasciando tuttavia spazio a spunti innovativi e a reinterpretazioni.

Elke Fleing

Adare Manor

Adare, Limerick, Ireland

The gigantic grounds belonging to Adare Manor include the spacious park, well-kept gardens, a formal French garden, wonderful old trees as well as the Maigue River, which is famous throughout Ireland for its trout. The formal garden with its geometric patterns shaped from box trees was designed by P. C. Hardwick around 1850. Another worthy sight is the majestic Lebanon cedar on the bank of the river. It is about 350 years old.

Auf dem riesigen Gelände, das zum Herrenhaus von Adare gehört, befinden sich neben dem weitläufigen Park gepflegte Gärten, ein formaler Französischer Garten, wunderbare alte Bäume sowie der Fluss Maigue, der in ganz Irland für seine Forellen berühmt ist. Der formale Garten mit den geometrischen, in Buchsbaum ausgeführten Mustern wurde um 1850 von P. C. Hardwick entworfen. Bemerkenswert ist auch die etwa 350 Jahre alte, majestätische, libanesische Zeder am Flussufer.

Le domaine immense qui appartient au Manoir Adare comprend le vaste parc, des jardins bien entretenus, un jardin à la française, de magnifiques vieux arbres et la rivière Maigue, réputée dans toute l'Irlande pour ses truites. Le jardin à la française avec ses topiaires de buis géométriques a été dessiné aux environs de 1850 par P. C. Hardwick. Un cèdre du Liban majestueux sur la berge de la rivière, âgé de 350 ans, vaut aussi le coup d'œil.

En el inmenso recinto perteneciente a la mansión de Adare, además de un extenso parque y cuidados jardines, encontramos un jardín formalista francés, magníficos árboles viejos y hasta el río Maigue, conocido en toda Irlanda por sus truchas. El diseño del jardín formalista, con sus setos de boj de líneas geométricas, fue obra de P. C. Hardwick allá por 1850. Cabe destacar igualmente el majestuoso cedro del Líbano a orillas del río, de unos 350 años de antigüedad.

Sull'enorme terreno che appartiene alla casa padronale di Adare, accanto all'ampio parco, si trovano dei giardini curati, un giardino francese formale, fantastici alberi secolari e il fiume Maigue, che è famoso in tutta l'Irlanda per le sue trote. Il giardino formale con i disegni geometrici creati dal bosso è stato progettato intorno al 1850 da P. C. Hardwick. Degno di nota è anche il maestoso cedro libanese sulla sponda del fiume, vecchio di circa 350 anni.

Formal gardens are as much part of Adare Manor as forests and parks.

Formale Gärten gehören ebenso zu Adare Manor wie Wälder und Parkanlagen.

Les jardins à la française appartiennent au Adare Manor, tout comme les forêts et les parcs.

Los jardines formalistas son tan propios de Adare Manor como sus bosques y parques.

I giardini formali fanno parte di Adare Manor come i boschi e i parchi.

16   Adare Manor *Adare, Limerick, Ireland*

The mighty Lebanon cedar with its wide spreading branches inspires awe. Two-hundred-year-old beech trees, araucaria, cork oak, aspen and blossoming cherry trees are also part of the admirable park, captivating nature-lovers.

Die mächtige libanesische Zeder mit ihren weit auskragenden Ästen flößt Ehrfurcht ein. Zweihundertjährige Buchen, Araukarien, Korkeichen, Espen und blühende Kirschbäume gehören ebenfalls zu der bewundernswerten Anlage und bezaubern Naturliebhaber.

Le puissant cèdre du Liban avec ses larges branches étalées inspire le respect. Les hêtres bicentenaires, les araucaria, les chêne-liège, les trembles, et les cerisiers en fleurs font aussi partie de ce parc admirable et charment les amoureux de la nature.

El magnífico cedro del Líbano, con sus ramas extendidas, impone respeto. Hayas de doscientos años, araucarias, alcornoques, álamos y cerezos en flor pertenecen igualmente a este maravilloso lugar y fascinan al amante de la naturaleza.

L'imponente cedro libanese con i suoi rami molto sporgenti impone rispetto. Faggi bicentenari, araucarie, querce da sughero, pioppi tremoli e ciliegi in fiore fanno anch'essi parte del bellissimo complesso e ammaliano gli amanti della natura.

The French garden with its geometric patterns leads from the austerity of the imposing stone building into nature. A small number of colourful flowers add variety to the colour range, which is dominated by green of all shades.

Der Französische Garten mit seinen geometrischen Mustern leitet von der Strenge des imposanten steinernen Gebäudes in die Natur über. Einige wenige bunte Blüten sorgen für Abwechslung in der Farbskala, die von Grün in allen Schattierungen beherrscht wird.

Le jardin à la française avec ses motifs géométriques crée un lien entre l'austérité de l'imposant bâtiment en pierre et la nature. Un petit nombre de fleurs colorées offrent une variété dans la gamme des couleurs, principalement dominée par les nuances de vert.

El jardín francés, de líneas geométricas, sirve de transición entre la sobriedad del imponente edificio de piedra y la naturaleza. Unas pocas flores de color dan vida a la paleta cromática, dominada por el verde en todas sus tonalidades.

Il giardino francese con i suoi disegni geometrici passa dal rigore dell'imponente edificio di pietra alla natura. Pochi fiori colorati creano un avvicendamento nella scala dei colori, che viene dominata dal verde in tutte le sue sfumature.

Arley Hall & Gardens
Northwich, Cheshire, England

Since the creation of today's contemporary gardens in 1846, Arley Hall has represented English garden design at its utmost perfection. Breathtaking colours, fine plant collections and a wonderful country house ambiance characterize the different garden rooms including the "Flag Garden", which earns its name from a paved inner sanctum, and a fish garden with a small pond, sundial circle, "Furlong Walk", the kitchen garden and arbour walk, winter garden, herb garden and scented garden. Not to be forgotten is the Ilex Avenue with 14 evergreen oaks clipped into giant cylinders.

Seit der Erschaffung der heutigen Anlagen 1846 stehen die Gärten von Arley Hall für englische Gartenkunst in Perfektion. Prächtige Farben, eine üppige Bepflanzung und ein wunderschöner ländlicher Charakter bestimmen die vielen verschiedenen Gartenräume: Den nach seinen Steinfliesen benannten „Flag Garden", einen Wasserfall, den Fischgarten mit einem Teich, den Sonnenuhr-Zirkel, den „Achtelmeilen"-Weg, den Küchengarten und den Laubengang, den Wintergarten, den Kräuter- und Duftgarten sowie die Ilex Avenue mit 14 zylindrisch beschnittenen Steineichen.

Depuis la création des jardins contemporains en 1846, le domaine d'Arley Hall illustre la perfection du jardin à l'anglaise. Des couleurs à couper le souffle, une végétation luxuriante et une merveilleuse ambiance champêtre caractérisent les différents espaces comprenant le « Flag Garden » qui tient son nom d'un espace intérieur pavé, le jardin aux poissons avec un bassin, le cadran solaire, la promenade d'un furlong, le potager et la promenade sous la tonnelle, le jardin d'hiver, le jardin aromatique et parfumé, ainsi que l'Avenue Ilex bordée de 14 chênes verts taillés en cylindres.

Desde la creación de los jardines contemporáneos en 1846, los jardines de Arley Hall son muestra del diseño de jardines ingleses en su máxima perfección. Colores impresionantes, una vegetación exuberante y un maravilloso ambiente campestre determinan los numerosos espacios ajardinados, incluyendo "Flag Garden", que obtiene su nombre de su baldosa, el jardín con estanque de peces, círculo de reloj solar, el "Furlong Walk", el jardín de cocina y el sendero de hojarasca, el jardín de invierno, el jardín de hierbas y aromas, así como la Ilex Avenue con 14 encinas podadas cilíndricamente.

Da quando, nel 1846, furono creati gli attuali giardini, Arley Hall è sinonimo di arte inglese del giardinaggio assolutamente perfetta. Colori straordinari, una vegetazione rigogliosa e un ambiente deliziosamente rurale fanno da cornice alle varie aree del giardino: il "Flag Garden", così chiamato per le piastrelle ornamentali, il giardino dei pesci con lo stagno, la meridiana, "Furlong Walk", il giardino delle cucine con le arcate, il giardino d'inverno, il giardino delle erbe e dei profumi e l'Ilex Avenue con 14 lecci cilindrici.

Today's stately home at Arley Hall was built between 1832 and 1845 and on the same site as the first house, dating from the 15th century.

Zwischen 1832 und 1845 entstand das heutige Herrenhaus von Arley Hall anstelle eines Vorgängerbaus aus dem 15. Jahrhundert.

L'actuel manoir d'Arley Hall fut construit entre 1832 et 1845 sur l'emplacement de l'ancien bâtiment datant du 15ème siècle.

La casa señorial actual de Arley Hall fue construida entre 1832 y 1845 en el mismo lugar en el que se encontraba la edificación original, del siglo XV.

L'attuale dimora di Arley Hall fu costruita tra il 1832 e il 1845 al posto di un precedente edificio del XV secolo.

The double herbaceous border, one of the highlights of the garden parterres, is regarded as one of the oldest of its kind in Great Britain (left).

Die doppelte Staudenrabatte, einer der Höhepunkte der Gartenanlage, gilt als eine der ältesten ihrer Art in Großbritannien (links).

La double plate-bande de vivaces, l'un des points de mire du jardin, est considérée comme l'une des plus anciennes de ce type en Grande-Bretagne (à gauche).

El doble arriate de arbustos, uno de los puntos álgidos del jardín, está considerado como uno de los más antiguos de su categoría de Gran Bretaña (izquierda).

Le doppie aiuole di piante perenni, una delle attrazioni del giardino, sono tra le più antiche della Gran Bretagna (a sinistra).

Bantry House
Bantry, Cork, Ireland

In 1997, the current owners began to restore the estate to its 1830 design. The garden structure was first planned by the Earl of Bantry using sketchbooks which he compiled travelling on the continent. The house, garden and landscape were to merge seamlessly. The land around the house was terraced, with Bantry House sitting on the third of seven terraces. Four terraces with an Italian garden and fountain were created to the south of the house, thus connecting the site with the wild woodland.

1997 begannen die heutigen Eigentümer den Garten in seiner Struktur der 1830er-Jahre wiederherzustellen. Diese Anlage hatte der Earl of Bantry nach Skizzen anlegen lassen, die er während Reisen auf dem Kontinent angefertigt hatte. Haus, Garten und Landschaft sollten dabei zu einer Einheit verschmelzen. Das Gelände um das Haus wurde in sieben Terrassen angelegt und Bantry House selbst auf der dritten Terrasse errichtet. Südlich des Hauses schließen sich vier Terrassen mit einem italienischen Garten mit Springbrunnen an und verbinden das Anwesen mit der Wildnis des Waldes.

En 1997, les actuels propriétaires commencèrent à restituer au jardin sa structure des années 1830. Le Comte de Bantry avait fait aménager ce domaine d'après les croquis qu'il avait dessinés au cours de ses voyages sur le continent. La maison, le jardin et le paysage devaient dégager une impression de continuité. L'espace autour de la maison fut aménagé en terrasses et la maison construite au niveau de la troisième terrasse. Quatre terrasses avec un jardin à l'italienne et une fontaine font la transition au sud de la maison entre le domaine et la forêt naturelle.

En 1997 los actuales propietarios del jardín comenzaron a recuperar su estructura de la década de 1830. La estructura del jardín fue proyectada originariamente por el conde de Bantry utilizando esbozos realizados durante sus viajes por el continente. La casa, el jardín y el paisaje debían fusionarse creando una sola unidad. El terreno que rodeaba la casa fue aterrazado, colocando la propia Bantry House en la tercera terraza de las siete existentes. Se crearon cuatro terrazas con un jardín italiano y una fuente en la cara sur de la casa, enlazando el edificio con el bosque silvestre.

Nel 1997 gli attuali proprietari iniziarono a restituire al giardino la struttura originale del 1830. Il giardino fu fatto allestire dal conte di Bantry in base a schizzi eseguiti da lui stesso durante i suoi viaggi in continente. La casa, il giardino e il paesaggio dovevano fondersi in un tutt'uno. La zona intorno alla casa fu suddivisa in sette terrazze, sulla terza delle quali venne costruita Bantry House. A sud di essa, altre quattro terrazze si aprono in un giardino italiano con fontane, collegando la tenuta alla natura e al bosco.

In summer, the wisteria circle around the fountain offers refreshing shade.

Im Sommer spendet das Glyzinienrondell um den Springbrunnen kühlen Schatten.

En été, la rotonde de glycine dispense une ombre fraîche autour de la fontaine.

En verano, el círculo de glicinas que bordean la fuente otorga una refrescante sombra.

In estate, il glicine che circonda la fontana regala ombra e fresco.

*The **"Hundred Steps"**, a stone staircase set amidst the estate and surrounded by rhododendrons and azaleas.*

*Die **„Hundert Stufen"**, eine steinerne Treppe, die den gesamten Garten durchzieht, sind gesäumt von Rhododendren und Azaleen.*

*Les **« cent marches »**, un escalier de pierre qui traverse tout le jardin, sont bordées de rhododendrons et d'azalées.*

*Los **"cien escalones"**, una escalera de piedra que cruza todo el jardín, están rodeados por rododendros y azaleas.*

*I **"cento scalini"**, una scalinata di pietra che attraversa tutto il giardino, sono fiancheggiati da rododendri e da azalee.*

Barrington Court
Barrington, Somerset, England

Barrington Court is one of the last gardens created according to formal plans made by the famous garden designer, Gertrude Jekyll (1843–1932). The 16th century Tudor manor house, built from local sandstone, is surrounded by various walled gardens: the kitchen garden is still cultivated today and produce used in Strode House restaurant. The garden includes an arboretum and lily pond with sunken garden of lilies, and the white garden with roses and iris. Intriguing brick-paved garden paths are an additional highlight.

Barrington Court gehört zu den letzten Gärten, für die die berühmte Gartengestalterin Gertrude Jekyll (1843–1932) Bepflanzungspläne entwarf. Um das Herrenhaus aus dem 16. Jahrhundert, errichtet aus heimischem Sandstein, gliedert sich der Garten in verschiedene Walled Gardens: In den heute noch bewirtschafteten Küchengarten, dessen Erträge im Restaurant im Strode House genossen werden können, das Arboretum, den Liliengarten am Teich, das abgesenkte Seerosenbecken sowie den weißen Garten mit Rosen und Iris. Die interessanten Pflaster aus Ziegelstein bilden ein weiteres Highlight.

Barrington Court est l'un des derniers jardins réalisé à partir de plans faits par la célèbre architecte paysagiste Gertrude Jekyll (1843–1932). Le manoir du 16ème siècle, construit avec le grès de la région, est entouré de plusieurs jardins clos. Il y a le potager qui est encore cultivé et dont les produits sont dégustés dans le restaurant de Strode House, l'arboretum, le bassin de nénuphars avec un boulingrin planté de lys et le jardin blanc avec des roses et des iris. Les allées pavées de briques sont une des originalités du jardin.

Barrington Court es uno de los últimos jardines planificados por la famosa paisajista y diseñadora de jardines Gertrude Jekyll (1843–1932). Alrededor de la casa señorial del siglo XVI construida de piedra arenisca, el jardín se distribuye en diferentes áreas amuradas: el jardín de cocina aún se utiliza hoy en día, y sus productos pueden probarse en el restaurante de Strode House. El jardín incluye un arboreto y un jardín de lirios sumergidos en el estanque, el jardín de nenúfares, y el jardín blanco con rosas e iris. Los interesantes pavimentos de ladrillo son otro de sus puntos estelares.

Barrington Court è uno degli ultimi giardini realizzati dalla celebre progettista Gertrude Jekyll (1843–1932). Attorno alla dimora del XVI secolo, costruita in arenaria locale, il giardino si sviluppa in diversi Walled Gardens: l'orto, tuttora coltivato, i cui prodotti si possono gustare nel ristorante della Strode House, l'arboreto, il giardino dei gigli con lo stagno, il bacino delle ninfee, situato più in basso, il giardino bianco, il roseto e il giardino degli iris. L'interessante pavimentazione in laterizio costituisce un'ulteriore attrazione.

Many areas clearly show Gertrude Jekyll's influence, for instance, natural planting with perennials which she selected in harmonious colours.

Viele Bereiche lassen deutlich den Einfluss Gertrude Jekylls spüren, die natürlich wirkende Pflanzungen mit Stauden in harmonierenden Farben propagierte.

De nombreux endroits illustrent l'influence de Gertrude Jekyll, comme les massifs colorés de vivaces où règne une merveilleuse harmonie de couleurs.

Numerosas áreas muestran una clara influencia de Gertrude Jekyll, como la plantación de aire natural con plantas perennes seleccionadas con colores que armonizan.

Molte aree tradiscono chiaramente l'influsso di Gertrude Jekyll, che diffuse le piante perenni, dall'effetto molto naturale, accostando sapientemente i colori.

The white garden—a visual link of the manor house with stables—simultaneously creates an atmosphere of tranquillity fused with a playful design.

Der weiße Garten, der optisch das Herrenhaus mit den Ställen verbindet, strahlt gleichzeitig Ruhe und Verspieltheit aus.

Le jardin blanc qui crée une transition visuelle entre le manoir et les étables dégage à la fois sérénité et gaieté folâtre.

El jardín blanco, que une estéticamente la casa señorial con las cuadras, irradia simultáneamente calma y un aire juguetón.

Il giardino bianco, che collega visivamente la dimora e le stalle, ispira allo stesso tempo serenità e allegria.

The Beth Chatto Gardens

Colchester, Essex, England

Beth Chatto began to design her inspirational garden in 1960. From an overgrown wasteland with poor soil and boggy hollows, she created a garden that wonderfully harmonizes with the surrounding countryside. Beth Chatto's motto was to treat problem zones as an advantage. Today, therefore, this garden offers a host of inspiring ideas for planting and garden design suited for dry or extremely wet gardens, poor soil, and water or woodland gardens. The specialized plant collections at the adjoining plant nursery are adapted to deal with all the imaginable challenges of garden design.

1960 begann Beth Chatto aus überwuchertem Wildland mit mageren Böden und sumpfigen Senken ihren inspirierenden Garten zu gestalten, der wunderbar mit der umgebenden Landschaft harmoniert. Beth Chattos Motto lautet: Betrachte Problemzonen als Vorteil. Und so bietet dieser Garten heute unzählige Pflanz- und Gestaltungsanregungen für trockene oder sehr feuchte Gärten, nährstoffarme Böden, Wasser- oder Waldgärten. Die angeschlossene Baumschule ist spezialisiert auf Pflanzen für alle denkbaren Problemfälle in der Gartengestaltung.

Quand Beth Chatto commença en 1960 d'aménager ce jardin si inspirant, ce n'était qu'une terre envahie par les mauvaises herbes sur des sols maigres et un bassin marécageux. Sa création est en parfaite harmonie avec le paysage environnant car sa devise était de considérer toute zone à problème comme un avantage. C'est pourquoi son jardin offre aujourd'hui d'innombrables idées de plantations et de conception pour des jardins secs ou très humides, des sols pauvres, des jardins d'eau ou boisés. La pépinière spécialisée attenante propose les plantes adaptées à tous les problèmes que l'on peut rencontrer dans l'aménagement d'un jardin.

Beth Chatto comenzó a diseñar su inspirador jardín en 1960. De una tierra pobre y hondonadas cenagosas en las que proliferaban plantas silvestres, dio forma a un jardín que armoniza maravillosamente con el paisaje colindante. El lema de Beth Chatto era considerar las zonas problemáticas como ventajas. Es por ello que, en la actualidad, este jardín ofrece un sinnúmero de ideas inspiradoras de jardinería y paisajismo para jardines secos o extremadamente húmedos, tierras pobres y jardines acuáticos o forestales. El centro forestal adyacente está especializado en el cuidado de plantas con todo tipo de problemas de jardinería.

Nel 1960, da un arido terreno selvatico coperto di erbacce, disseminato di avvallamenti paludosi, Beth Chatto creò un suggestivo giardino in perfetta armonia con il paesaggio circostante. Considerare le zone problematiche come un vantaggio era il motto di Beth Chatto: oggi qui si trovano innumerevoli proposte per l'allestimento di giardini aridi o molto umidi, terreni poveri, giardini d'acqua o boschivi. Il vicino vivaio di piante arboree è specializzato nel trattamento di tutti i problemi riguardanti l'allestimento dei giardini.

Against a backdrop of old oaks, waterloving plants such as reeds, knotgrass, butterbur and arum lilies create a picturesque scene around water.

Vor dem Hintergrund alter Eichen fügen sich feuchtigkeitsliebende Pflanzen wie Schilfe, Knöterich, Pestwurzeln und Zantedeschien malerisch um einen Teich.

Avec de vieux chênes en toile de fond, les plantes qui se plaisent dans l'eau comme les roseaux, les renouées, les pétasites et les arums d'Éthiopie forment un écrin pittoresque autour de l'étang.

Robles centenarios en el fondo, plantas amantes de la humedad como cañas, espérgulas, petasites y lirios de agua crean un paisaje pintoresco alrededor de un estanque.

Sullo sfondo di un antico querceto, piante amanti dell'acqua come canne, persicarie, petasiti e gigli del Nilo creano un pittoresco insieme intorno allo stagno.

Bodnant

Tal-y-Cafn, Conwy, Wales

Whilst the 81.25-acre garden is now a National Trust property, the Aberconway family, the creators of Bodnant Garden since 1875, still own the surrounding estate. The garden has two main areas: an upper formal level comprising lawns and borders with five terraces around the house and a lower, more natural area called The Dell with steeply sided banks formed by the valley of the River Hiraethlyn. The garden is famous for its 180-ft long Laburnum Arch, waterfall, and exceptional plant collections.

Während der 325.000 m² große Garten heute im Besitz des National Trust ist, nennt die Familie Aberconway, seit 1875 die Gestalter von Bodnant Garden, den umliegenden Grundbesitz noch immer ihr Eigen. Es gibt zwei Hauptbereiche: Einen oberen formalen Teil mit Rasen und Rabatten auf fünf Terrassen um das Herrenhaus herum und den unteren, natürlicheren Bereich, genannt „The Dell", mit steilen, durch den Fluss Hiraethlyn gebildeten Ufern. Der Garten ist berühmt für seinen 55 Meter langen Bogengang aus Goldregen, den Wasserfall und eine außergewöhnliche Pflanzenvielfalt.

C'est aujourd'hui le National Trust qui en est le propriétaire de ce jardin couvrant quelque 325.000 m², mais la famille Aberconway, créatrice de Bodnant Garden depuis 1875, possède toujours le domaine environnant. Le jardin a deux parties principales : un plan supérieur formel avec pelouses et parterres sur cinq terrasses autour du manoir et un plan inférieur, étendu, plus naturel appelé « The Dell », délimité par les berges pentues de la rivière Hiraethlyn. Le jardin est réputé pour sa tonnelle de cytises longue de 55 mètres, sa cascade et l'exceptionnelle diversité de ses plantes.

Mientras que actualmente el jardín de una extensión aproximada de 325.000 m² es propiedad del National Trust, la familia Aberconway, creadora de los jardines Bodnant Garden desde 1875, sigue siendo la propietaria de los terrenos colindantes. El jardín consta de dos áreas principales: un nivel formal superior que comprende praderas y arriates con cinco terrazas que rodean la casa residencial, y otra área inferior, más natural, llamada "The Dell", con orillas empinadas formadas por el valle del río Hiraethlyn. El jardín es famoso por su arcada de lluvia de oro de 55 metros de longitud, la cascada y una inusitada variedad vegetal.

Il giardino di circa 325.000 mq appartiene oggi al National Trust, mentre la tenuta circostante è ancora di proprietà della famiglia Aberconway, che sin dal 1875 allestisce Bodnant Garden. È formato da due aree principali: una superiore, allestita in modo formale, con prati e aiuole disposti su cinque terrazze, che circonda la dimora, e una inferiore, più naturale, chiamata "The Dell", scoscesa e delimitata dal fiume Hiraethlyn. Il giardino è celebre per l'arcata di maggiociondolo, lunga 55 metri, la cascata e la straordinaria varietà di piante.

50   Bodnant *Tal-y-Cafn, Conwy, Wales*

52   Bodnant *Tal-y-Cafn, Conwy, Wales*

Bodnant *Tal-y-Cafn, Conwy, Wales* 53

Buckfast Abbey

Buckfastleigh, Devon, England

The idyllic gardens, partly modelled on medieval plans, are an impressive example of monastic horticulture and garden design. The many lawned areas are complemented by three self-contained gardens: the lavender garden, sensory garden, which is based on designs for medieval pleasure gardens, and physic garden, divided into four zones and containing over 200 plants. Another, fourth area, which is separated from visitors by a moat, partially includes poisonous medicinal plant collections that are still used today.

Die zum Teil nach mittelalterlichem Vorbild angelegten idyllischen Gärten sind ein eindrucksvolles Beispiel klösterlicher Gartenbaukunst. Neben vielen Grünflächen findet man drei in sich geschlossene Themengärten: den Lavendelgarten, den Garten der Sinne, der auf Entwürfen mittelalterlicher Lustgärten basiert, und den in vier Bereiche unterteilten Heilgarten mit über 200 Pflanzen. Ein vierter Bereich, durch einen Graben vom Besucher abgetrennt, beherbergt teilweise giftige Heilpflanzen, die noch heute verwendet werden.

Ces jardins idylliques, dont les plans sont en partie basés sur ceux du Moyen-Âge, sont un exemple impressionnant de l'horticulture monastique. Le gazon est très présent ; trois espaces distincts dévoilent des thèmes différents : le jardin de lavande, le jardin sensoriel qui repose sur des dessins de jardins des plaisirs médiévaux et le jardin médicinal, divisé en quatre parties, totalisant plus de 200 variétés de plantes. Une quatrième section, séparée des visiteurs par un fossé, contient des espèces de plantes vénéneuses dont certaines sont encore utilisées.

Los idílicos jardines modelados al estilo medieval, son un magnífico ejemplo de la jardinería monacal. Junto a las superficies verdes, encontramos tres jardines temáticos cerrados: el jardín de lavanda, el jardín de los sentidos, basado en los diseños de los jardines medievales de recreo, y el jardín curativo, dividido en cuatro áreas, con más de 200 variedades de plantas. Otra zona, la cuarta, separada de visitantes por un foso, alberga algunas plantas curativas venenosas, que aún se utilizan en la actualidad.

Questi idilliaci giardini, in parte realizzati secondo il gusto medioevale, sono uno straordinario esempio di architettura da giardino di tipo monastico. Oltre a molti prati, vi sono tre giardini a tema a se stanti: il giardino della lavanda, il giardino dei sensi, basato su schizzi che ritraevano i giardini medievali delle delizie, e il giardino officinale, suddiviso in quattro aree, con più di 200 piante. Una quarta area, separata dai visitatori tramite un fossato, contiene, tra le altre, piante officinali velenose tuttora utilizzate.

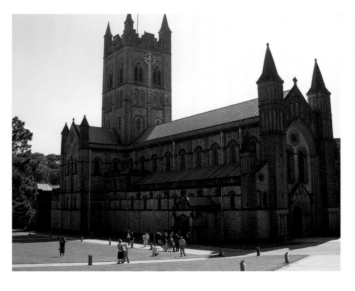 

The gardens are deliberately designed as a frame for, rather than a distraction from, the church of the Abbey founded in 1018.

Die Gärten lenken bewusst nicht von der Kirche ab, die im Zentrum der 1018 gegründeten Abtei liegt.

Le dessin des jardins a pour but de ne pas éloigner le visiteur de l'église dressée au centre du site de cette abbaye fondée en 1018.

Los jardines han sido diseñados deliberadamente para realzar la iglesia de la abadía construida en 1018.

Volutamente, la struttura dei giardini non distoglie l'attenzione dalla chiesa che si trova al centro dell'abbazia fondata nel 1018.

56   Buckfast Abbey *Buckfastleigh, Devon, England*

The scented lavender garden contains about 150 varieties of the plant, illustrating the diversity of this species, which was also used in medieval times as an antiseptic.

Der duftende Lavendelgarten präsentiert etwa 150 verschiedene Arten und somit die Vielfalt dieser Gattung, die im Mittelalter auch als Antiseptikum diente.

Le jardin de lavande au parfum envoûtant compte quelque 150 variétés de plantes aromatiques et illustre la diversité des espèces qui servaient d'antiseptiques au Moyen Âge.

El aromático jardín de lavanda presenta unas 150 variedades diferentes, ilustrando la diversidad de la planta, que en la Edad Media se utilizaba como antiséptico.

Il profumato giardino della lavanda ospita circa 150 diverse specie di questa pianta, utilizzata nel Medioevo anche come antisettico.

Chirk Castle

Chirk, Wrexham, Wales

The award-winning garden surrounding the majestic medieval castle offers a variety of attractions: the woodland walk through a medieval hunting park, a lime tree avenue dating from the 17th century, perennials and herbaceous borders with many rare plants, a biotope for numerous invertebrates, a rock garden and terrace with a stunning panoramic view of the neighbouring counties. Chirk Castle presents exquisite craftsmanship and architecture spanning several centuries. Good examples of its charm are the ironwork entrance gates made by the Davies brothers in 1719.

Der preisgekrönte Garten rund um die mächtige mittelalterliche Burg bietet viele Attraktionen: den bewaldeten mittelalterlichen Jagdpark, die Lindenallee aus dem 17. Jahrhundert, Staudengarten und -rabatten mit vielen seltenen Pflanzen, ein Biotop für wirbellose Tiere, einen Steingarten und eine Terrasse mit überwältigendem Ausblick über die umliegenden Grafschaften. Handwerks- und Baukunst aus mehreren Jahrhunderten tragen zu Chirk Castles Reiz bei, zum Beispiel die schmiedeeisernen Eingangstore, 1719 von den Brüdern Davies angefertigt.

Ce jardin, souvent primé, entourant un majestueux château fort, offre de nombreuses attractions : un parc de chasse médiéval boisé, une allée de tilleuls datant du 17ème siècle, des parterres de vivaces et des plate-bandes de vivaces avec de nombreuses espèces rares, un biotope pour les invertébrés, un jardin de rocaille et une terrasse avec une vue époustouflante sur les comtés voisins. Plusieurs siècles d'artisanat d'art et d'architecture font le charme de Chirk Castle, comme par exemple le portail en fer forgé, œuvre des frères Davies en 1719.

El jardín galardonado con varios premios que rodea el magnífico castillo medieval ofrece grandes atracciones: el parque de caza medieval situado en un bosque, la avenida de tilos que data del siglo XVII, jardines y arriates de arbustos con numerosas especies vegetales singulares, un biotopo para numerosos invertebrados, un jardín rocoso y una terraza con una impresionante vista de los condados adyacentes. El Castillo de Chirk presenta exquisitas obras de artesanía y arquitectura de varios siglos. Algunos buenos ejemplos de su encanto son las puertas de hierro forjado elaboradas por los hermanos Davies en 1719.

Il premiato giardino che circonda l'imponente fortezza medievale ha molte attrazioni: il boscoso parco di caccia medievale, il viale di tigli del XVII secolo, i giardini e le aiuole con rare piante perenni, il biotopo per gli animali invertebrati, il giardino alla giapponese e la terrazza da cui si gode la splendida vista delle contee circostanti. Artigianato e architettura di epoche diverse, come i cancelli di ingresso in ferro battuto, risalenti al 1719 e opera dei fratelli Davies, fanno di Chirk Castle un luogo incantevole.

The magnificent ironwork gates were commissioned by Sir Richard Myddelton in 1711/12 and bear his coat-of-arms.

Die reich verzierten eisernen Tore entstanden 1711/12 im Auftrag von Sir Richard Myddelton, dessen Wappen sie krönt.

Le portail en fer forgé richement ouvragé fut réalisé en 1711/12 à la demande de Sir Richard Myddelton dont il porte les armoiries.

Las engalanadas puertas de hierro fueron encargadas en 1711/12 por Sir Richard Myddelton, y llevan su escudo de armas.

I cancelli di ferro riccamente lavorati risalgono al 1711/12 e sono stati eseguiti su ordine di Sir Richard Myddelton, di cui recano lo stemma.

A typical feature of 19th century garden design: yew topiaries, clipped into shape, and used to structure the space.

Typisch für die Gartengestaltung im 19. Jahrhundert: Eiben wurden, in Form geschnitten, als Elemente zur Raumgliederung gepflanzt.

Élément typique de l'agencement des jardins au 19ème siècle : une topiaire d'ifs, véritable sculpture végétale, ponctuait l'espace.

Características típicas de la jardinería del siglo XIX: los tejos podados, plantados a modo de elemento estructurador del espacio.

Un elemento tipico dei giardini del XIX secolo erano i tassi ornamentali che strutturavano l'ambiente.

Chirk Castle *Chirk, Wrexham, Wales* 65

Chirk Castle *Chirk, Wrexham, Wales* 67

Compton Castle
Marldon, Paignton, Devon, England

Compton Castle, the last fortified castle in Devon, was home for most of the past 600 years to the Gilbert family. The family's most famous members were Sir Humphrey Gilbert, who established the colony of Newfoundland, and his half-brother, Sir Walter Raleigh. The castle, which is heavily defended by a medley of towers and battlements, was built in three parts between 1340 and 1520. The gardens, enclosed by a stone curtain wall, have an imposing rose garden and luscious flowerbeds as well as a knot garden, typical for the Elizabethan period, and with perfectly designed parterres.

Compton Castle, das letzte in der Grafschaft Devon gebaute befestigte Schloss, ist seit 600 Jahren fast ununterbrochen im Besitz der Familie Gilbert. Ihre berühmtesten Mitglieder sind Humphrey Gilbert, Begründer der Kolonie Neufundland, und sein Halbbruder Sir Walter Raleigh. Gebaut wurde das stark befestigte Herrenhaus in drei Abschnitten zwischen 1340 und 1520. Die Gartenanlage, umschlossen von einer steinernen Mauer, besticht durch einen Rosengarten und viele Blumen sowie einen für die Elisabethanische Epoche typischen Knotengarten mit musterförmig angelegten Beeten.

Compton Castle, le dernier des châteaux forts construits dans le comté du Devon, appartient à la famille Gilbert depuis pratiquement 600 ans. Ses membres les plus connus sont Humphrey Gilbert, qui établit la colonie de Terre-Neuve, et son demi-frère, Sir Walter Raleigh. Le château, massivement fortifié, fut construit en trois parties entre 1340 et 1520. Dans les jardins, entourés d'un mur de pierre, le visiteur est frappé par la roseraie et la profusion de fleurs, ainsi que par le jardin de nœuds, typique de l'époque élisabéthaine, avec ses parterres au dessin régulier.

El castillo de Compton, el último castillo fortificado en el condado de Devon, fue el hogar de la familia Gilbert durante prácticamente los últimos 600 años. Sus miembros más conocidos eran Humphrey Gilbert, fundador de la colonia de Terranova, y su hermanastro, Sir Walter Raleigh. El castillo fue convertido en fortaleza en tres fases, entre 1340 y 1520. Los jardines, rodeados de un muro de piedra, están compuestos por un impresionante jardín de rosas e innumerables flores, así como un jardín de nudos típico de la época isabelina, con parterres perfectamente diseñados.

Compton Castle, l'ultimo castello fortificato costruito nella contea di Devon, appartiene da quasi 600 anni alla famiglia Gilbert, i cui membri più noti sono Humphrey Gilbert, fondatore della colonia di Terranova, e il suo fratellastro, Sir Walter Raleigh. La dimora, ben fortificata, fu costruita in tre fasi tra il 1340 e il 1520. Il parco, circondato da mura di pietra, ospita un meraviglioso roseto e un'infinità di fiori, nonché un giardino "a nodo", tipico dell'epoca elisabettiana, con aiuole disposte a formare particolari disegni.

An enchanting view of a profusion of plants almost makes you forget that Compton Castle was a heavily defended fortress.

Beim Anblick dieser verspielten Bepflanzung kann man fast vergessen, dass Compton Castle eine gut bewehrte Festung war.

La vue enchanteresse d'un tel foisonnement de plantes fait presque oublier que Compton Castle était une forteresse bien défendue.

Admirando esta encantadora composición de plantas uno casi olvida que el castillo de Compton fue una auténtica fortaleza.

La vista di questo giocoso giardino fa dimenticare che Compton Castle era una fortezza ben attrezzata.

70   Compton Castle *Marldon, Paignton, Devon, England*

The knot garden is framed by box hedges, orthogonally planned flowerbeds and box trees clipped into spiral shapes (p. 70 and below).

Der Knotengarten mit von Buchs gerahmten, quadratischen Beeten und knotenartig geschnittenen Buchsbäumen (S. 70 und unten).

Le jardin de noeuds est composé de parterres orthogonaux encadrés de massifs de buis et de buis taillés en spirale (p. 70 et en bas).

El jardín de nudos enmarcado en bojs, arriates cuadrados y bojs recortados a modo de nudos (pág. 70 y abajo).

Il giardino a nodo con aiuole quadrate orlate di bosso e bossi potati a spirale (pag. 70 e sotto).

Compton Castle *Marldon, Paignton, Devon, England* 75

Crathes Castle

Banchory, Aberdeenshire, Scotland

The National Trust for Scotland now manages Crathes Castle, owned for over 350 years by the Burnetts of Leys. The castle grounds contain about 530 acres of woodlands and fields. The garden is divided into eight themed areas on the basis of geometric design. Sybil Burnett developed the gardens and was heavily influenced in the 1920s by the garden designer, Gertrude Jekyll. The gardens are famous for their colour and themed arrangement: the parterres include a white, red and golden garden as well as a rose garden.

Crathes Castle, mehr als 350 Jahre im Besitz der Familie Burnett of Leys, ist heute in der Obhut des National Trust for Scotland. Das rund 2 km² große Grundstück ist teilweise bewaldet. Der Garten ist geometrisch in acht unterschiedliche Bereiche geteilt. Bei der Weiterentwicklung der Gärten ließ sich Sybil Burnett in den 1920er-Jahren stark von der Gartendesignerin Gertrude Jekyll inspirieren. Sie sind berühmt für ihre Farb- und Themensortierung und umfassen einen weißen, roten und goldenen Garten sowie einen Rosengarten.

Crathes Castle, propriété de la famille Burnett of Leys pendant plus de 350 ans, est désormais géré par le National Trust for Scotland. Le domaine qui s'étend sur environ 2 km² est en partie couvert de forêts. Le jardin est divisé en huit espaces distincts géométriques. Quand Sybil Burnett développa les jardins dans les années 1920, elle se laissa grandement influencer par l'architecte paysagiste Gertrude Jekyll. Ceux-ci sont réputés pour leur aménagement par couleur et par thème et comprennent un jardin blanc, rouge et doré ainsi qu'une roseraie.

El castillo Crathes, desde hace más de 350 años propiedad de la familia Burnett of Leys, actualmente es propiedad del National Trust for Scotland. Las tierras del castillo abarcan unos 2 km² de campos y bosques. El jardín está dividido geométricamente en ocho áreas temáticas diferentes. Sybil Burnett desarrolló los jardines y se dejó influenciar por el diseñador de jardines Gertrude Jekyll en los años 20 del siglo XX. Son famosos por su clasificación cromática y temática, e incluyen un jardín blanco, rojo y dorado, así como un jardín de rosas.

Crathes Castle, per più di 350 anni di proprietà della famiglia Burnett of Leys, è oggi sotto la custodia del National Trust for Scotland. La tenuta, di circa 2 kmq, è in parte coperta da boschi. Il giardino è suddiviso geometricamente in otto aree differenti. L'ulteriore sviluppo, voluto negli anni venti da Sybil Burnett, ha subìto il forte influsso della progettista di giardini Gertrude Jekyll. Le sezioni sono suddivise in base al colore e al tema e includono un giardino bianco, uno rosso e uno dorato, nonché un roseto.

The red (far left) and golden garden (p. 77)—two areas designed according to the colours of the plant collections.

Der rote (ganz links) und der goldene Garten (S. 77), zwei der nach Farben geordneten Gartenbereiche.

Le jardin rouge (tout à gauche) et le jardin doré (p. 77), deux des espaces aménagés en fonction de la couleur des plantes.

El jardín rojo (izquierda extrema) y el dorado (pág. 77), dos áreas de jardín clasificadas por colores.

Il giardino rosso (a sinistra) e quello dorato (pag. 77), due delle sezioni suddivise in base al colore.

78   Crathes Castle *Banchory, Aberdeenshire, Scotland*

One of the garden's highlights: the "June Border", the largest herbaceous border, and regarded as one of the finest borders in Scotland.

Einer der Höhepunkte des Gartens: Die „June Border", das große „Juni-Staudenbeet", gilt als eines der schönsten in Schottland.

Une des attractions du jardin: la « June Border », la grande plate-bande de vivaces fleuries en juin, est considérée comme l'une de plus belles d'Écosse.

Uno de los puntos estelares del jardín: "June Border", el gran "arriete de arbustos de junio" está considerado como uno de los más bellos de Escocia.

Una delle maggiori attrazioni del giardino è "June Border", la grande aiuola di piante perenni di giugno, una delle più belle della Scozia.

80   Crathes Castle Banchory, Aberdeenshire, Scotland

Crathes Castle *Banchory, Aberdeenshire, Scotland* 81

Denmans Garden

Denmans Lane, Fontwell, West Sussex, England

John Brookes MBE, an internationally renowned and multi-award winning garden designer, as well as author of several standard books on horticultural design, created a perfect example of his personal style in his private, almost 4-acre garden. Denmans Garden is a contemporary garden full of ideas that come to life in a combination of foliage forms, colours and textures. The garden contains over 1,500 perennials and collections of shrubs, which create diverse effects: from romantic, tamed wilderness to artfully planned, organic patterns.

Mit seinem privaten, fast 1,6 Hektar großen Garten liefert John Brookes MBE, ein international angesehener und mehrfach ausgezeichneter Gartengestalter und Autor mehrerer Standardwerke zum Thema, eine perfekte Visitenkarte seines persönlichen Stils. Denmans Garden ist ein zeitgenössischer Garten voller Ideen, der von der Kombination von Formen, Farben und Texturen lebt. Über 1.500 Staudenarten und Sträucher werden hier kultiviert und schaffen die unterschiedlichsten Effekte: von romantischer, gezähmter Natur bis hin zu künstlich angelegten Mustern.

John Brookes MBE, architecte paysagiste de renommée internationale, lauréat de nombreux prix et auteur prolifique d'ouvrages sur l'horticulture paysagère, livre dans son jardin privé de presque 1,6 hectare un exemple parfait de son style personnel. Denmans Garden est un jardin contemporain fourmillant d'idées qui vivent de la combinaison des formes, des couleurs et des textures. Plus de 1500 espèces de plantes vivaces et d'arbustes y sont cultivées, aboutissant à cette richesse d'atmosphères : nature romantique, apprivoisée ou motifs artistiquement dessinés.

Con su jardín privado de casi 1,6 hectáreas de superficie, John Brookes, Miembro de la Orden del Imperior Británico, jardinero renombrado y distinguido en numerosas ocasiones y autor de obras fundamentales sobre jardinería, presenta la tarjeta de visita perfecta de su estilo personal. El jardín de Denmans es un jardín contemporáneo rebosante de ideas que toman cuerpo mediante formas, colores y texturas. Incluye más de 1.500 especies perennes y arbustos que crean distintos efectos: desde motivos románticos de la delicada naturaleza, hasta patrones artísticos planificados por la mano del hombre.

Con il suo giardino privato di circa 1,6 ettari, John Brookes MBE, un progettista di giardini di fama internazionale più volte premiato e autore di varie opere standard sul tema, fornisce un eccellente biglietto da visita del proprio stile personale. Denmans Garden è un giardino contemporaneo pieno di idee, che vive della combinazione di forme, colori e tessiture. Vi vengono coltivati oltre 1.500 tipi di piante perenni e arbusti che creano effetti diversi: dalla natura romantica e mite alle composizioni create ad effetto.

1001 ideas: the garden layout is divided into many small areas—a casual, jungly effect yet with formal structure, or fine planting and tamed wilderness.

1001 Ideen: Viele kleine Gartenräume prägen das Bild — mal luftig und formal, mal dicht bepflanzt und wild.

Un millier d'idées: le parc s'articule en petits espaces jardinés — tantôt aérés et formels, tantôt luxuriants et sauvages.

Mil y una ideas: numerosas pequeñas áreas caracterizan el espacio; a veces con un efecto formal y airoso, otras bien pobladas y silvestres.

1001 idee: tanti piccoli spazi-giardino caratterizzano l'ambiente che appare ora arioso e formale, ora rigoglioso e selvaggio.

86   Denmans Garden *Denmans Lane, Fontwell, West Sussex, England*

Denmans Garden *Denmans Lane, Fontwell, West Sussex, England*   87

Denmans Garden *Denmans Lane, Fontwell, West Sussex, England*

Indigenous and *exotic plants are harmoniously combined to create an inspiring, complete artwork.*

Einheimische und *exotische Pflanzen sind harmonisch kombiniert und lassen ein stimmiges Gesamtkunstwerk entstehen.*

Les plantes *indigènes et exotiques sont harmonieusement combinées pour créer un ensemble artistique homogène.*

Plantas autóctonas *y exóticas combinadas armoniosamente para dar lugar a una obra de arte completa de lo más inspiradora.*

Piante locali *ed esotiche sono accostate sapientemente creando un'opera d'arte di grande armonia.*

Exbury Gardens
Southampton, Hampshire, England

The creator of the 250-acre landscape garden was none other than Lionel de Rothschild. His passion for rhododendrons produced new plant collections with the personal development of 1,210 hybrid varieties. Exbury is colourful in spring, with azaleas, magnolias, primroses, camellias and bluebells all surrounded by rare tree species. The garden also has a path lined with hydrangeas, a rock garden, exotic sundial garden, three ornamental ponds and water cascades.

Der Erschaffer des 102 Hektar großen Landschaftsgartens war niemand Geringeres als Lionel de Rothschild. Er spezialisierte sich so erfolgreich auf die Zucht von Rhododendren, dass ihm die Züchtung von 1.210 Hybriden gelang. Exbury erstrahlt im Frühling mit seinen Azaleen, Magnolien, Primeln, Kamelien und Hasenglöckchen, umgeben von seltenen Baumarten, in voller Farbenpracht. Der Garten verfügt auch über einen von Hortensien gesäumten Weg, einen Steingarten, den exotischen Sonnenuhr-Garten, drei ornamentale Teiche und Wasserkaskaden.

Le créateur de ce jardin paysager de 102 hectares n'était rien moins que Lionel de Rothschild. Passionné par les rhododendrons, il se spécialisa dans leur culture et parvint à élever 1210 variétés hybrides. Au printemps, Exbury resplendit de la floraison des azalées, magnolias, primevères, camélias et campanules de toutes les couleurs qu'entourent des essences d'arbres rares. Le parc possède également un sentier bordé d'hortensias, un jardin de rocaille, un jardin exotique avec un cadran solaire, trois bassins ornementaux et des cascades.

El creador del jardín paisajístico de 102 hectáreas no fue otro que Lionel de Rothschild. Su pasión por los rododendros dio lugar a nuevas colecciones de plantas, desarrollando 1.210 variedades híbridas. Exbury irradia color en primavera, con azaleas, magnolias, primaveras, camelias y jacintos, rodeados de especies de árboles poco frecuentes. El jardín también dispone de un sendero orlado de hortensias, un jardín rocoso, un exótico jardín de reloj solar, tres estanques ornamentales y cascadas de agua.

A creare questo giardino all'inglese di 102 ettari è stato il celebre Lionel de Rothschild. Egli si specializzò nella coltivazione del rododendro con tale successo da riuscire a creare 1.210 specie ibride. In primavera, Exbury si presenta in tutto il suo splendore tra azalee, magnolie, primule, camelie e giacinti di mille colori, attorniati da alberi rari. Il giardino ha anche un sentiero orlato di ortensie, un giardino giapponese, un giardino della meridiana esotico, tre stagni ornamentali e cascate.

At Exbury, rhododendrons, azaleas and camellias flower in a profusion of colour during April and May.

Im April und Mai blühen in Exbury die Rhododendren, Azaleen und Kamelien in einem prachtvollen Farbenrausch.

En avril et en mai, les rhododendrons, les azalées et les camélias fleurissent à Exbury dans une profusion de couleurs.

En abril y mayo, en Exbury florecen rododendros, azaleas y camelias dando lugar a una enorme explosión de color.

In aprile e in maggio fioriscono a Exbury rododendri, azalee e camelie dai meravigliosi colori.

Alongside natural woodland and unspoilt areas, Exbury also has formally designed gardens, such as the Sundial Garden.

In Exbury finden sich neben waldähnlichen, natürlich wirkenden Gebieten auch formal gestaltete Bereiche wie der Sonnenuhr-Garten.

A Exbury, des espaces boisés à l'aspect naturel côtoient des jardins de conception formelle, tel que le jardin au cadran solaire.

Junto a las áreas forestales de aspecto natural, Exbury también integra jardines diseñados formalmente como el jardín del reloj solar.

Accanto a zone boschive dall'aspetto naturale, a Exbury si trovano aree allestite in modo formale, come il giardino della meridiana.

Falkland Palace

Falkland, Fife, Scotland

Members of the royalty used to enjoy pastimes such as archery, royal tennis and falconry in the estate grounds of this Renaissance palace. Falconry is still practised and the oldest tennis court dating from 1539 is still in use today. The colourful garden is divided into four areas: the Keepers Lawn, the Rose Garden following and emphasizing the lines of the Great Hall, the Percy Cane Garden below with lawns and herbaceous borders, the Lily Pond Garden enclosed by yew hedges and the orchard planted in the 17th century.

Einst vertrieb sich der Adel seine Zeit in der Parkanlage des Renaissance-Schlosses mit Bogenschießen, Royal Tennis und Falknerei. Die Falknerei und der älteste noch immer bespielte Tennisplatz von 1539 bestehen auch heute noch. Der farbenfrohe Garten gliedert sich in vier Bereiche: den so genannten „Keepers Lawn", den Rosengarten entlang der großen Halle, den darunter liegenden, mit Rasen und Staudenbeeten bepflanzten Percy Cane Garden und den von Eibenhecken und dem im 17. Jahrhundert angelegten Obstgarten umgebenen Garten mit Seerosenteich.

Jadis les aristocrates s'adonnaient à leurs passe-temps dans le parc de ce château Renaissance : tir à l'arc, tennis et fauconnerie. La fauconnerie se pratique toujours et le plus ancien court de tennis datant de 1539 est encore en service de nos jours. Le jardin plein de couleurs est divisé en quatre secteurs : la « Keepers Lawn », la roseraie longeant la grande halle, le Percy Cane Garden situé en deçà, avec ses pelouses et parterres de vivaces et le jardin au bassin de nymphéas, entouré de haies d'ifs et d'un verger planté au 17ème siècle.

Los miembros de la nobleza solían disfrutar en el tiro con arco, el tenis real y la cetrería de las tierras de este palacio renacentista. La cetrería y la más antigua pista de tenis, de 1539, que aún se utilizan hoy en día. Los jardines rebosantes de color se dividen en cuatro áreas: los llamados "Keepers Lawn", el jardín de rosas a lo largo de la gran sala, el jardín Percy Cane con césped y arrietes de arbustos, así como el jardín de árboles frutales del siglo XVII con estanque de nenúfares rodeado de setos de tejo.

Un tempo i nobili trascorrevano le giornate nel parco del castello rinascimentale tirando con l'arco, giocando alla pallacorda o praticando la caccia con il falcone. La falconiera e il campo da tennis più antico, ancora in uso, risalente al 1539, sono tuttora presenti. Il variopinto giardino è suddiviso in quattro aree: il cosiddetto "Keepers Lawn", il roseto che fiancheggia il salone, il sottostante Percy Cane Garden, con prati e aiuole di piante perenni, e il giardino con lo stagno delle ninfee, circondato da siepi di tassi e dal frutteto del XVII secolo.

Built between 1450 and 1541 under James IV and James V, the castle at the foot of the Lomond Hills was the family seat of the Stuarts for over 200 years.

Entstanden zwischen 1450 und 1541 unter James IV und James V, war das Schloss am Fuß der Lomond Hills über 200 Jahre lang Residenz der Familie Stuart.

Construit entre 1450 et 1541 sous les rois James IV et James V, le château au pied de la colline de Lomond fut pendant 200 ans la résidence de la famille Stuart.

Construido entre 1450 y 1541 bajo los reinados de Jacobo IV y Jacobo V, el palacio situado a los pies de Lomond Hills fue la sede familiar de la familia Stuart durante más de 200 años.

Costruito tra il 1450 e il 1541 sotto Giacomo IV e Giacomo V, il castello ai piedi delle colline Lomond Hills fu per 200 anni la residenza della famiglia Stuart.

Long stretches of magnificent-flowering herbaceous borders in all colours define the garden's essential character.

Viele Meter lange Staudenbeete in allen Farben bestimmen den Charakter eines Großteils des Gartens.

Les longues plates-bandes de vivaces de toutes les couleurs sont l'une des caractéristiques majeures du jardin.

Arrietes de arbustos de varios metros, de todos los colores, definen el carácter esencial del jardín.

Lunghe aiuole di piante perenni di tutti i colori caratterizzano gran parte del giardino.

Hannah Peschar Sculpture Garden

Ockley, Surrey, England

When Hannah Peschar acquired the Tudor cottage and garden in 1978, her garden was completely overgrown. Inspired by a visit to the Dutch Kröller-Müller Museum and its sculpture garden, in 1984, the art dealer decided to transform her own garden into a sculpture park that would be open to the public. Peschar's husband, the landscape designer, Anthony Paul, then started to plan a green setting for a changing exhibition of artworks by contemporary artists that were to be showcased amid the plant collections.

Als Hannah Peschar 1978 das Cottage aus der Tudorzeit und den dazugehörigen Garten erwarb, war dieser völlig verwahrlost. Inspiriert durch einen Besuch im holländischen Kröller-Müller-Museum und dessen Skulpturengarten, beschloss die Kunsthändlerin 1984, ihren eigenen Garten ebenfalls in einen Skulpturenpark zu verwandeln und dem Publikum zu öffnen. Peschars Mann, der Landschaftsdesigner Anthony Paul, schuf in der Folgezeit einen grünen Rahmen für die stetig wechselnden Werke zeitgenössischer Künstler, die durch die Bepflanzung besonders zur Geltung kommen.

Quand Hannah Peschar fit l'acquisition en 1978 de ce cottage datant de l'époque des Tudor et du jardin attenant, celui-ci était à l'abandon. Inspirée par une visite du Musée néerlandais Kröller-Müller et de son jardin de sculptures, l'artiste décida en 1984 de transformer son propre parc en jardin de sculptures et de l'ouvrir au public. Le mari d'Hannah Peschar, l'architecte paysager Anthony Paul, créa donc un écrin de verdure où sont exposées des œuvres d'artistes contemporains renouvelées régulièrement et mises en valeur par la végétation environnante.

Cuando Hannah Peschar adquirió el castillo de la época de los Tudor y su jardín en 1978, estaba totalmente abandonado. Inspirada por una visita al museo holandés Kröller-Müller y sus jardines esculturales, la comerciante de objetos de arte decidió transformar su propio jardín en un parque con esculturas en 1984, y abrirlo al público. Su marido, el paisajista Anthony Paul, comenzó entonces a crear el marco verde para las exposiciones temporales de artistas contemporáneos, que destacan especialmente entre las colecciones de plantas.

Quando fu acquistato da Hannah Peschar, nel 1978, il cottage di epoca Tudor era del tutto fatiscente. Ispirata da una visita al museo olandese Kröller-Müller e al suo giardino di sculture, nel 1984 la commerciante d'arte decise di trasformare in un parco di sculture anche il proprio giardino e di aprirlo al pubblico. Suo marito, il progettista di paesaggi Anthony Paul, realizzò in seguito uno scenario verde per le opere d'arte contemporanee che si avvicendavano nell'esposizione e che la vegetazione valorizzava in modo particolare.

The many large ponds in the water garden reflect the sculptures amid the rich green foliage, thus creating a magical atmosphere.

Viele Weiher in diesem Wassergarten reflektieren das üppige Grün und die Skulpturen und schaffen eine mystische Atmosphäre.

Les nombreux étangs de ce jardin d'eau reflètent les sculptures au sein de la verdure et créent une atmosphère mythique.

Los numerosos estanques de este jardín acuático reflejan las esculturas que asoman entre el rico follaje verde, creando un ambiente mágico.

I molti specchi d'acqua di questo giardino acquatico riflettono il verde carico e le sculture creando un'atmosfera mistica.

Hannah Peschar's sculpture garden was the first of its kind in England and paved the way for many others to create similar gardens.

Hannah Peschars Skulpturengarten war der erste seiner Art in England und bereitete so den Weg für viele Nachahmer.

Avec son jardin de sculptures, le premier de ce type en Angleterre, Hannah Peschar fut précurseur et ouvrit la voie à d'autres créations similaires.

El jardín escultural de Hannah Peschar fue el primero de su categoría de Inglaterra y abrió el camino a numerosos jardines similares.

Il giardino delle sculture di Hannah Peschar, il primo di questo genere in Inghilterra, ha aperto la strada a molte imitazioni.

Hestercombe Gardens

Cheddon Fitzpaine, Taunton, Somerset, England

Hestercombe contains three very different gardens spanning three centuries of garden design and created by the most respected designers of their time. The 18th century landscape garden was the creation of Coplestone Warre Bampfylde, the formal Victorian Terrace (dating from the 1870s) and the Edwardian Formal Garden, for which the arts and crafts architect, Sir Edwin Lutyens and Gertrude Jekyll collaborated on plans and plant collections. This garden is considered one of the finest preserved examples of this creative duo's work and today is Grade I-listed on the English Heritage Gardens Register.

Hestercombe verfügt über drei sehr unterschiedliche Gärten aus drei Jahrhunderten, die von den angesehensten Gartengestaltern ihrer Zeit angelegt wurden: Den von Coplestone Warre Bampfylde im 18. Jahrhundert geschaffenen Landschaftsgarten, die aus den 1870er-Jahren stammende, formal bepflanzte viktorianische Terrasse und den formalen Garten, den Arts-and-Crafts-Architekt Sir Edwin Lutyens und Gertrude Jekyll in der edwardianischen Epoche schufen. Letzterer gilt als eines der schönsten erhaltenen Beispiele dieser Zusammenarbeit und steht heute unter Denkmalschutz.

Hestercombe abrite trois jardins très différents qui enjambent trois siècles de conception paysagère et furent créés par les paysagistes les plus estimés de leur époque. Le jardin paysager du 18ème siècle est l'œuvre de Coplestone Warre Bampfylde. L'architecte d'art et d'artisanat Sir Edwin Lutyens conçut le jardin formel de style édouardien et confia à Gertrude Jekyll les plantations de ce jardin et de la terrasse victorienne remontant aux années 1870. Ce jardin est considéré comme l'un des plus beaux exemples de leur collaboration et aujourd'hui classé au patrimoine des monuments historiques.

Hestercombe alberga tres jardines muy diferentes de tres siglos creados por los paisajistas de mayor renombre de sus tiempos: el jardín paisajista de Coplestone Warre Bampfylde del siglo XVIII, la terraza victoriana, de la década de 1870, y el jardín formal de la época eduardiana del arquitecto de Bellas Artes Sir Edwin Lutyens y Gertrude Jekyll. Este último es uno de los ejemplos más bellos conservados de su colaboración, y en la actualidad es patrimonio cultural de Inglaterra.

Hestercombe accoglie tre giardini diversissimi risalenti a tre secoli differenti, realizzati dagli architetti più apprezzati del loro tempo: il giardino all'inglese di Coplestone Warre Bampfylde, del XVIII secolo, la terrazza vittoriana allestita in modo formale negli anni 70 del XIX secolo, e il giardino formale, realizzato in epoca edoardiana dall'architetto Arts and Crafts Sir Edwin Lutyens e da Gertrude Jekyll. Quest'ultimo è uno dei più begli esempi della loro collaborazione e si trova oggi sotto la protezione delle Belle Arti.

The landscape garden is designed to given the impression of an idealized classical landscape with temples, grottoes and lakes.

Der Landschaftsgarten sollte ein Idealbild klassischer Landschaften mit Tempeln, Grotten und Seen sein.

Le jardin paysager incarne l'idéal du paysage classique avec temples, grottes et étangs.

El jardín paisajista fue diseñado para dar la impresión de un paisaje clásico idealizado con templos, grutas y lagos.

Il giardino all'inglese si ispira all'immagine ideale dei paesaggi classici con tempietti, grotte e specchi d'acqua.

116   Hestercombe Gardens *Cheddon Fitzpaine, Taunton, Somerset, England*

The Edwardian Formal Garden, designed in 1903, was restored in 1973 when a chance discovery was made of Gertrude Jekyll's original plans.

Der 1903 entworfene edwardianische Garten wurde 1973 nach den zufällig gefundenen Originalplänen Gertrude Jekylls restauriert.

Le jardin de style édouardien conçu en 1903 fut restauré en 1973 après qu'on eut retrouvé par hasard les plans originaux de Gertrude Jekyll.

El jardín formal eduardiano, diseñado en 1903, fue restaurado en 1973 cuando se descubrieron los planos originales de Gertrude Jekyll por azar.

Il giardino edoardiano progettato nel 1903 fu restaurato nel 1973 sulla base dei piani originali di Gertrude Jekyll, rinvenuti casualmente.

118   Hestercombe Gardens *Cheddon Fitzpaine, Taunton, Somerset, England*

Inverewe Garden

Poolewe, Highland, Scotland

In 1864, Osgood Mackenzie acquired a craggy plot of land—known as "Ploc Ard" or "The High Lump"—on Scotland's north-western coast. With immense patience and at great financial expense, he took several decades to create a paradise for exotic plants that flourish in the mild, Gulf Stream climate. He transported tons of soil and waited 20 years before continuing with planting, until the Scots pines, which he personally planted, gave sufficient wind shelter. Today, the garden hosts a variety of plants from all around the world.

Osgood Mackenzie erwarb 1864 ein äußerst karges Stück Land an der Nordwestküste Schottlands, „Ploc Ard" oder „The High Lump" genannt. Mit sehr viel Geduld und finanziellem Aufwand schuf er hier über mehrere Jahrzehnte ein exotisches Pflanzenparadies, das durch das milde Klima des Golfstroms begünstigt wurde. Er ließ tonnenweise Erde herbeischaffen und wartete mit der weiteren Bepflanzung 20 Jahre, bis die von ihm gepflanzten Schottischen Pinien ausreichend Windschutz boten. Heute bietet der Garten eine Pflanzenvielfalt aus aller Welt.

En 1864, Osgood Mackenzie acquit, sur la côte nord-ouest de l'Écosse, un terrain particulièrement aride appelé « Ploc Ard » ou « The High Lump ». Avec une patience infinie et des moyens financiers considérables, il créa là en quelques décennies un paradis pour les plantes exotiques qui bénéficient de la douceur du climat due au gulf stream. Il fit apporter des tonnes de terre et attendit vingt ans avant de continuer à planter, jusqu'à ce que les pins écossais qu'il avait lui-même plantés offrent une protection contre le vent suffisante. Aujourd'hui, le jardin cultive une grande diversité de plantes du monde entier.

En 1864, Osgood Mackenzie adquirió un pobre pedazo de tierra situado en la costa noroeste de Escocia, conocido como "Ploc Ard" o "The High Lump". Con una enorme paciencia y un elevado coste económico, se tardaron varias décadas en crear un paraíso de plantas exóticas favorecido por el suave clima de la corriente del golfo. Hizo traer toneladas de tierra y esperó 20 años hasta empezar a plantar, una vez que los pinos escoceses plantados por él mismo, proporcionaron la protección suficiente del viento. Actualmente, el jardín presenta una gran serie de plantas procedentes de todo el mundo.

Nel 1864 Osgood Mackenzie acquistò sulla costa nord-occidentale della Scozia un appezzamento di terreno estremamente brullo, chiamato "Ploc Ard" o "The High Lump". Con molta pazienza e grande sforzo finanziario, nel corso di parecchi decenni realizzò qui un esotico paradiso floreale, favorito dal clima mite della corrente del Golfo. Vi lasciò trasportare tonnellate di terra, e attese 20 anni prima di iniziare la coltivazione di altre piante, affinché i pini scozzesi da lui stesso piantati offrissero sufficiente protezione dai venti. Oggi il giardino dispone di una grande varietà di piante di ogni parte del mondo.

The most important plants are cultivated in the sheltered Walled Garden, situated directly by the beach: Chinese rhododendrons, Tasmanian Eucalyptus, flowers, vegetables and climbing fruit trees.

Im direkt am Strand gelegenen Walled Garden sind windgeschützt die wichtigsten Pflanzen platziert: Chinesische Rhododendren, tasmanischer Eukalyptus, Blumen, Gemüse und Spalierobst.

Les plantes les plus importantes sont cultivées à l'abri du vent dans un jardin fermé, situé directement au bord de la plage : rhododendrons chinois, eucalyptus de Tasmanie, fleurs, légumes et arbres fruitiers en espalier.

En Walled Garden, situado junto a la playa, se encuentran las plantas más importantes, protegidas del viento: rododendros chinos, eucaliptos tasmanos, flores, hortalizas y frutos de parra.

Direttamente sulla spiaggia, il Walled Garden ospita, in posizione protetta dal vento, le piante più importanti: rododendri cinesi, eucalipti della Tasmania, fiori, verdure e frutta a spalliera.

A large part of Inverewe Garden is an arboretum. Here, you can see a host of diverse rhododendrons as well as plant collections from New Zealand, Tasmania, Chile and South Africa.

Ein Großteil von Inverewe Garden bildet ein Arboretum. Hier findet man neben einer Vielzahl unterschiedlicher Rhododendren Pflanzen aus Neuseeland, Tasmanien, Chile und Südafrika.

Une grande partie du parc d'Inverewe est un arboretum. On y trouve, aux côtés de différentes espèces de rhododendrons, des collections de plantes de Nouvelle-Zélande, de Tasmanie, du Chili et d'Afrique du sud.

Gran parte del jardín Inverewe forma un arboreto. En él pueden encontrarse, junto a un gran número de distintos rododendros, plantas procedentes de Nueva Zelanda, Tasmania, Chile y Sudáfrica.

Gran parte di Inverewe Garden è costituita da un arboreto. Oltre a numerosi rododendri, vi si trovano piante originarie della Nuova Zelanda, della Tasmania, del Cile e del Sudafrica.

Inverewe Garden *Poolewe, Highland, Scotland*   125

126   Inverewe Garden *Poolewe, Highland, Scotland*

Lanhydrock
Bodmin, Cornwall, England

The picturesque manor house is situated in the middle of a 890-acre country estate on the River Fowey. The house is surrounded by a horseshoe-shaped garden with formal Victorian flowerbeds and herbaceous borders. On the hillside, the garden has an exceptional collection of trees and shrubs, including magnolias, camellias and hydrangeas. In 1914, Lady Clifden planted the exquisite flowerbeds, forming a crescent. In 1971, the National Trust closed up the crescent, creating a full circle by adding additional beds and hedges.

Das malerische Herrenhaus liegt inmitten eines 360 Hektar großen Geländes am River Fowey. Ein hufeisenförmiger Garten mit formal gestalteten viktorianischen Blumenparterren und Staudenrabatten umgibt es. Der angrenzende Hügel ist mit ausgewählten Bäumen und Sträuchern bepflanzt, darunter Magnolien, Kamelien und Hortensien. Lady Clifden legte 1914 spektakuläre Blumenbeete an, die einen Halbkreis bildeten. 1971 schloss der National Trust diesen Halbkreis durch weitere Beete und Hecken zum Vollrund.

Le pittoresque manoir se dresse au centre d'un domaine de 360 hectares sur les bords de la rivière Fowey. Il est entouré d'un jardin en fer à cheval avec des plates-bandes de fleurs et de vivaces, d'inspiration victorienne, soigneusement dessinés. La butte attenante est plantée d'arbres et d'arbustes sélectionnés parmi lesquels figurent magnolias, camélias et hortensias. En 1914, Lady Clifden dessina de superbes parterres fleuris en croissant. En 1971, le National Trust ferma le croissant et ajouta d'autres haies et parterres pour en faire un cercle.

La pintoresca casa señorial está situada en medio de un terreno de 360 hectáreas a orillas del río Fowey. La rodea un jardín en forma de herradura con parterres florales de forma victoriana y arrietes de arbustos. La colina colindante incluye una selección de árboles y matorrales, entre los que se encuentran magnolias, camelias y hortensias. En 1914, Lady Clifden plantó exquisitos parterres florales que formaban un semicírculo. En 1971, el National Trust rodeó este semicírculo con otros arriates y setos completando el círculo.

La pittoresca dimora sorge in una tenuta di 360 ettari sul fiume Fowey, circondata da un giardino a forma di ferro di cavallo con un parterre di fiori e aiuole di piante perenni, di gusto vittoriano, allestiti in maniera formale. La collina adiacente è ricoperta di alberi e arbusti selezionati, tra cui magnolie, camelie e ortensie. Nel 1914 Lady Clifden vi piantò spettacolari aiuole di fiori che formavano un semicerchio. Nel 1971 il National Trust chiuse il semicerchio con altre aiuole e siepi, creando un insieme di forma circolare.

Lanhydrock is among Cornwall's most beautiful stately homes. The garden design retains its 19th century structure.

Lanhydrock gehört zu den schönsten Herrenhäusern Cornwalls. Sein Garten hat die Gestalt des 19. Jahrhunderts bewahrt.

Lanhydrock compte parmi les plus belles demeures de Cornouailles. Le jardin a conservé sa structure du 19ème siècle.

Lanhydrock es una de las casas señoriales más bellas de Cornualles. Su jardín ha mantenido el diseño del siglo XIX.

Lanhydrock è una delle più belle dimore della Cornovaglia. Il suo giardino ha conservato l'aspetto del XIX secolo.

130　Lanhydrock *Bodmin, Cornwall, England*

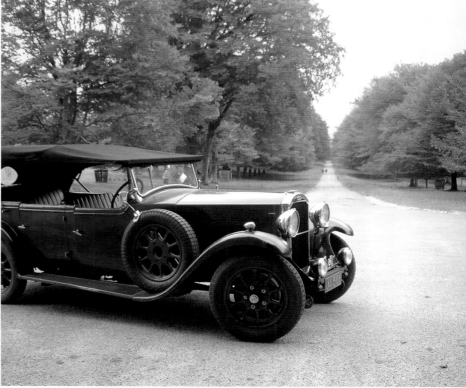

132   Lanhydrock *Bodmin, Cornwall, England*

Bronze vases decorate the floral parterres and were transported here in 1857, originally from Bagatelle Chateau in Paris.

Die Blumenparterre zieren Vasen aus Bronze, die 1857 hierher gebracht wurden und aus Schloss Bagatelle in Paris stammen.

Les parterres fleuris sont ornés de vases de bronze amenés ici en 1857 en provenance du château de Bagatelle à Paris.

El parterre floral se ornamenta con floreros de bronce que fueron traídos en 1857 desde el castillo Bagatelle de París.

Il parterre di fiori è ornato da vasi in bronzo provenienti dal castello Bagatelle di Parigi e portati qui nel 1857.

Mottisfont Abbey Garden
near Romsey, Hampshire, England

William Briwere, among others, advisor to Richard the Lionheart, established the Augustinian priory in 1201, which William Sandys transformed in the 15th century into a country mansion. After a varied history, the National Trust took over the estate in 1972. Today, Mottisfont is world famous for its old-fashioned rose collection, with 300 flourishing varieties. Part of the rose garden originates from the private collection of its creator, Graham Stuart Thomas. The parkland and walled gardens are well worth a visit.

William Briwere, u. a. Berater von Richard Löwenherz, gründete 1201 die Augustinerabtei, die im 15. Jahrhundert von William Sandys in ein Herrenhaus verwandelt wurde. Nach einer wechselvollen Geschichte übernahm 1972 der National Trust das Anwesen. Heute ist Mottisfont weltberühmt für seine Sammlung alter Rosensorten, von denen über 300 im Rosengarten blühen. Zum Teil stammen sie aus der privaten Sammlung von Graham Stuart Thomas, der diesen Bereich gestaltete. Aber auch die Parkanlagen und die Walled Gardens sind sehenswert.

William Briwere, qui fut, entre autres, conseiller de Richard Cœur de Lion, fonda en 1201 le prieuré augustinien dont William Sandys fit un manoir au 15ème siècle. À l'issue d'une histoire mouvementée, le National Trust reprit le domaine en 1972. Aujourd'hui, Mottisfont est mondialement connu pour sa collection de roses anciennes dont plus de 300 variétés fleurissent la roseraie. Certaines proviennent de la collection privée de son créateur, Graham Stuart Thomas. L'ensemble du parc et les jardins clos valent le déplacement.

William Briwere, entre otros, asesorador de Ricardo Corazón de León, fundó la abadía agustina en 1201, que fue transformada por William Sandys en una casa señorial en el siglo XV. Tras una variada historia, el National Trust se hizo cargo del lugar en 1972. En la actualidad, Mottisfont es famoso en el mundo entero por sus antiguas variedades de rosas, de las cuales más de 300 florecen en su jardín de rosas. Parcialmente provienen de la colección privada de Graham Stuart Thomas, que diseñó esta área. El parque y los jardines amurados también son dignos de visitar.

William Briwere, che fu anche consigliere di Riccardo Cuordileone, fondò nel 1201 un'abbazia agostiniana che nel XV secolo William Sandys trasformò in una dimora. Dopo molte peripezie, nel 1972 il National Trust rilevò la tenuta. Oggi Mottisfont è celebre in tutto il mondo per il roseto con oltre 300 diverse specie di rose. Esse provengono in parte dalla collezione privata di Graham Stuart Thomas, che ha allestito quest'area. Ma anche il parco e i Walled Gardens, sono degni di una visita.

The garden of the former priory has a long history, still visible today in a fine collection of old trees.

Der Garten der ehemaligen Abtei blickt auf eine lange Geschichte zurück — der alte Baumbestand zeugt noch heute davon.

Le jardin de l'ancien prieuré a une longue histoire — comme en témoignent les vieux arbres qui peuplent le parc.

El jardín de la antigua abadía tiene una larga historia, de la que aún son testigos algunos de sus árboles.

Il giardino di quella che un tempo era l'abbazia è carico di storia oggi raccontata dagli alberi secolari.

Mottisfont Abbey Garden *near Romsey, Hampshire, England*

Mottisfont Abbey Garden *near Romsey, Hampshire, England*   137

138   Mottisfont Abbey Garden *near Romsey, Hampshire, England*

Mottisfont Abbey Garden *near Romsey, Hampshire, England* 139

The building's different uses are visible from the different masonry of the external façades.

Die veränderte Nutzung des Gebäudes lässt sich von außen an der Verwendung unterschiedlicher Mauersteine ablesen.

Le bâtiment eut plusieurs fonctions, comme le montrent les différentes briques utilisées pour les façades.

Los diferentes usos del edificio se observan desde el exterior por la utilización de distintas fachadas.

Esternamente, l'utilizzo di mattoni di vario tipo indica i diversi usi a cui fu adibito l'edificio.

Osborne House & Gardens

East Cowes, Isle of Wight, England

In 1845, Queen Victoria and Prince Albert purchased Osborne House as a private family retreat. A new country house was built in Italian style complete with flagtower and about 50 acres of formal gardens with Italian influences, created partly using the well-established late 18th century facilities. With its terraces and ornamental parterres interspersed with statues representing the seasons, the fruit and flower gardens as well as park with rare tree species, this is one of the finest examples of Victorian garden design.

1845 kauften Queen Victoria und Prinz Albert Osborne House als private Rückzugsmöglichkeit. Ein neues Herrenhaus mit Turm im italienischen Stil wurde errichtet und auf rund 20 Hektar ein italienisch beeinflusster formaler Garten angelegt, der in Teilen auf eine Anlage des 18. Jahrhunderts zurückgeht. Mit seinen Terrassen mit ornamentalen Parterren und Statuen der Jahreszeiten, den Obst- und Blumengärten sowie dem Park mit seltenen Baumarten ist dies eines der schönsten Beispiele viktorianischer Gartenkunst.

En 1845 la Reine Victoria et le Prince Albert achetèrent Osborne House comme lieu de retraite familiale. Un nouveau manoir avec une tour du drapeau de style italien fut alors construit et un jardin formel avec des influences italiennes aménagé sur environ 20 hectares, reprenant en partie les arrangements du 18ème siècle. Avec ses terrasses et ses parterres ornementaux, ses statues des saisons, ses vergers et jardins de fleurs et son parc planté d'essences rares, le domaine est l'une des plus belles démonstrations de l'architecture paysagiste victorienne.

En 1845, la Reina Victoria y el Príncipe Alberto adquirieron Osborne House como refugio familiar. Construyeron una nueva mansión señorial de estilo italiano y crearon un jardín formal con influencias italianas de unas 20 hectáreas, inlcuyendo partes de un jardín del siglo XVIII. Con sus terrazas de parterres ornamentales y estatuas de las cuatro estaciones, los jardines florales y de árboles frutales, así como el parque de raras especies, es una de las muestras más bellas del arte paisajista victoriano.

Nel 1845 la regina Vittoria e il principe Alberto acquistarono Osborne House come dimora privata. Furono poi realizzati una nuova dimora con torre in stile italiano e un giardino formale di uguale ispirazione di circa 20 ettari, creati utilizzando in parte un parco del XVIII secolo. Le terrazze con i parterre ornamentali e le statue delle stagioni, i frutteti e i giardini fioriti, il parco con alberi rari fanno di Osborne House uno dei più begli esempi di architettura da giardino del periodo vittoriano.

Queen Victoria died at Osborne House in 1901, surrounded by the lovingly rebuilt and expanded Italian gardens and estate.

In dem von ihr aufwendig im italienischen Stil umgebauten und erweiterten Osborne Haus verstarb 1901 Queen Victoria.

La Reine Victoria mourut en 1901 à Osborne House, cette demeure qu'elle avait fait reconstruire et agrandir avec tant de soin dans le style italien.

La Reina Victoria falleció en 1901 en la mansión Osborne, reconstruida con mimo y complementada con jardines italianos ampliados.

La regina Vittoria morì nel 1901 a Osborne House, che lei stessa fece accuratamente ristrutturare e ampliare in stile italiano.

The Swiss Cottage was built in 1853 and furnished especially for the royal couple's children, where they could play and learn gardening skills—the children planted their own vegetable plot.

Das Schweizer Berghaus wurde 1853 speziell für die königlichen Kinder zum Spielen gebaut und möbliert. Im Garten ringsum bauten die Kinder ihr eigenes Gemüse an.

Le Swiss Cottage fut construit en 1853 et meublé spécialement pour les enfants du couple royal. Ceux-ci pouvaient jouer et apprendre le jardinage en plantant leurs propres légumes dans le jardin.

La casa de montaña suiza fue construida y amueblada especialmente para los niños de la realeza en 1853: cultivaban sus propias hortalizas alrededor del jardín.

La baita svizzera fu costruita e ammobiliata nel 1853 affinché i figli dei sovrani potessero giocarvi. Nel giardino circostante, i bambini piantavano le proprie verdure.

Portmeirion

Portmeirion, Gwynedd, Wales

Portmeirion has been developed from 1925 by Clough Williams-Ellis into a small Italianate resort village with a quirky mix of different architectural styles. Its unique location, on the Atlantic coast, means that in spring and summer the extensive park covering slopes is a glorious blend of brightly coloured flowers. Old trees, many planted in Victorian times, dominate the coastline with giant rhododendrons, azaleas and majestic magnolias. Two lakes and an attractive, formally structured entrance complete the garden.

Portmeirion entwickelte sich seit 1925 durch Clough Williams-Ellis zu einem kleinen Dorf mit italienischem Charakter, das mit seinen unterschiedlichen Baustilen einen charmanten Mix bildet. Seine Besonderheit liegt dabei in der unmittelbaren Nähe zum Atlantik. Im Frühjahr und Sommer ziert den ausgedehnten Park und seine Anhöhen eine vielfältige Blütenpracht. Viele alte Bäume, zum Teil noch aus viktorianischer Zeit, riesige Rhododendren, Azaleen und prächtige Magnolien bestimmen das Bild ebenso wie zwei Seen und der formal gestaltete Eingangsbereich.

Portmeirion se transforme depuis 1925 sous l'impulsion de Clough Williams-Ellis en un petit village de style italien avec un amusant mélange de différents styles d'architecture. Grâce à son emplacement unique, sur la côte atlantique, ce parc très étendu sur des pentes se pare au printemps et en été d'une multitude de fleurs multicolores. De nombreux arbres anciens, dont certains plantés à l'époque victorienne, des rhododendrons géants, des azalées et de superbes magnolias constituent le décor, complété par deux lacs et une entrée de conception formelle.

Portmeirion se ha ido desarrollando desde 1925 por Clough Williams-Ellis, hasta convertirse en un pequeño pueblo de aire italiano con una divertida mezcla de diferentes estilos arquitectónicos. Su ubicación, única, a orillas del Atlántico, permite que en primavera y verano el amplio parque repleto de pendientes se vea orlado por una exuberante colección de flores multicolores. Árboles centenarios, algunos de ellos plantados en tiempos victorianos, enormes rododendros, azaleas y majestuosas magnolias dominan el paisaje costero. Dos lagos y una atractiva entrada con estructura formal completan el jardín.

Dopo il 1925, grazie a Clough Williams-Ellis, Portmeirion divenne un villaggio di ispirazione italiana con un divertente insieme di stili architettonici differenti. La sua particolarità risiede nel fatto che si affaccia direttamente sull'Atlantico. L'esteso parco costellato di alture è ricoperto in primavera e in estate di fiori multicolori. Numerosi alberi secolari, alcuni addirittura di epoca vittoriana, rododendri giganteschi, azalee e splendide magnolie ne formano il paesaggio, insieme a due laghi e all'area di ingresso di stampo formale.

The summer residence, created in about 1850 and situated by the waterside, today houses a small hotel (right).

In einer um 1850 direkt am Wasser entstandenen Sommerresidenz ist heute ein kleines Hotel untergebracht (rechts).

La résidence d'été, édifiée au bord de l'eau, vers 1850, abrite aujourd'hui un petit hôtel (à droite).

La residencia estival, construida alrededor de 1850 justo en la orilla, es un pequeño hotel en la actualidad (derecha).

Nella residenza estiva, costruita intorno al 1850 direttamente sull'acqua, si trova oggi un piccolo hotel (a destra).

Warm enough for palms: not only the architectural style, but also the planting gives Portmeirion its Mediterranean flair.

Warm genug für Palmen: Nicht nur die Bebauung, auch die Bepflanzung vermittelt in Portmeirion mediterranes Flair.

Un climat assez chaud pour les palmiers: le style architectural mais aussi la végétation confèrent à Portmeirion un charme méditerranéen.

Calor suficiente para albergar palmeras: no sólo el estilo arquitectónico, sino también la flora, otorga a Portmeirion un aire mediterráneo.

La temperatura è ideale per le palme: architettura e vegetazione conferiscono a Portmeirion un fascino mediterraneo.

Powis Castle

Welshpool, Powys, Wales

Powis Castle, home to the Earls of Powis over five centuries, dates back to medieval times: the garden is world famous. The Italianate and French styling of the unique terrace overhung with large yew topiaries conceals some delightful surprises, for instance, a secret tunnel. The various features of this prize-winning garden are best discovered on a long walk. Enjoy the walled terraced gardens, attractive perennials, aviaries, 18th century statues and a Victorian orangery.

Der Garten der mittelalterlichen Burg Powis Castle, seit fünf Jahrhunderten Sitz der Earls of Powis, ist weltberühmt. Einzigartig ist besonders die Anlage des italienisch und französisch anmutenden, von riesigen formgeschnittenen Eiben überladenen Terrassengartens, der so manche Überraschung präsentiert, zum Beispiel einen geheimnisvollen Durchgang. Nur auf einem langen Spaziergang sind all die Bereiche dieser preisgekrönten Anlage zu entdecken: ummauerte Terrassengärten, Sträuchergärten, Vogelvolieren, Statuen aus dem 18. Jahrhundert und eine viktorianische Orangerie.

Le jardin de Powis Castle, forteresse médiévale et résidence des comtes de Powis depuis cinq cents ans, est mondialement connu. L'agencement particulier du jardin à la française et à l'italienne en terrasses que surplombe une énorme topiaire d'ifs recèle de délicieuses surprises, comme un tunnel secret. Seule une longue promenade permet de découvrir toutes les beautés de ce parc souvent primé: jardins clos en terrasses, massifs d'arbustes, volières, statues du 18ème siècle et orangerie victorienne.

Los jardines del castillo medieval de Powis, residencia de los condes de Powis desde hace cinco siglos, es famoso en el mundo entero. El estilo único de aire italiano y galo de la terraza cargada de tejos podados deleita con alguna que otra deliciosa sorpresa: por ejemplo, un túnel secreto. La mejor manera de descubrir todas las áreas de este jardín galardonado es dar un largo paseo: disfrute de jardines aterrazados limitados, jardines de arbustos, pajareras, estatuas del siglo XVIII y un invernáculo victoriano.

Il giardino che circonda la fortezza medievale di Powis Castle, da cinque secoli residenza dei conti di Powis, è celebre in tutto il mondo. A caratterizzarne il fascino unico sono soprattutto i giardini a terrazze di ispirazione italiana e francese, abbelliti da tassi ornamentali, che nascondono angoli inaspettati, come una misteriosa galleria. Solo una lunga passeggiata permette di scoprire tutte le meraviglie di questa tenuta: giardini a terrazza circondati da mura, giardini con cespugli, voliere, statue del XVIII secolo e un'orangerie vittoriana.

Thanks to *its position high on a rock, Powis Castle commands magnificent views towards England and the surrounding countryside.*

Bedingt durch *die erhöhte Lage hat man von Powis aus einen fantastischen Ausblick auf die umliegende Landschaft.*

Perché sur *un roc, Powis Castle offre une vue magnifique sur le paysage environnant.*

Gracias a *su elevada ubicación, Powis ofrece unas vistas maravillosas de los paisajes colindantes.*

Grazie alla *posizione sopraelevata, da Powis si gode un fantastico panorama.*

12th century *Powis Castle still looks like a fortress. The castle's rooms are filled with an exquisite collection of paintings, furniture and tapestries.*

Das um *1200 errichtete Powis Castle wirkt nur noch von außen wie eine Festung. Die Gemächer sind mit prachtvollen Gemälden, Möbeln und Tapisserien ausgestattet.*

Construit vers *l'an 1200, Powis Castle ressemble à une forteresse, mais seulement de l'extérieur. Les intérieurs recèlent en effet de splendides tableaux, meubles et tapisseries.*

El Castillo *de Powis, construido en torno al año 1200, aún tiene aspecto de fortaleza. Sus salas incluyen una exquisita colección de cuadros, muebles y tapices.*

Costruito attorno *al 1200, Powis Castle si presenta come una fortezza soltanto dall'esterno. Le sale sono arredate con dipinti, mobili e tappezzerie di gusto squisito.*

RHS Garden Wisley

Woking, Surrey, England

The design of the 240-acre estate at Wisley dates back to 1878 and "Oakwood experimental garden" created by George Ferguson Wilson with the aim of making 'difficult plants grow successfully'. In 1903, the garden was gifted to the Royal Horticultural Society and is one of the finest gardens in southern England, as well as a training and research centre. Today, an arboretum, orchid collection, stone and show garden are among the inspirational features, including the extensive glasshouse.

Die Gestaltung des 97 Hektar großen Areals von Wisley geht auf den 1878 von George Ferguson Wilson angelegten „Oakwood experimental garden" zurück, der der erfolgreichen Zucht schwieriger Pflanzen diente. Seit 1903 wurde Wisley durch die Royal Horticultural Society zu einer der großartigsten Anlagen Südenglands und zu einem angesehenen Ausbildungs- und Forschungszentrum ausgebaut. Heute sorgen u. a. ein Arboretum, eine Orchideensammlung, Stein- und Mustergärten sowie ein riesiges Gewächshaus für Inspiration.

L'élaboration des 97 hectares du domaine de Wisley remonte à 1878 et à l'« Oakwood experimental garden » créé par George Ferguson Wilson dans le but d'acclimater des plantes difficiles. Dès 1903, sous la houlette de la Royal Horticultural Society, Wisley devint un des parcs les plus admirables du sud de l'Angleterre mais aussi un centre de recherche et de formation. Aujourd'hui, un arboretum, une collection d'orchidées, un jardin de rocaille et d'exposition ainsi qu'une immense serre sont autant de sources d'inspiration.

El diseño del terreno de 97 hectáreas de Wisley se remonta a 1878, al "Oakwood experimental garden" creado por George Ferguson Wilson para conseguir cultivar con éxito plantas delicadas. Desde 1903, Wisley fue convertido por la Royal Horticultural Society en uno de los jardines más exquisitos del sur de Inglaterra, así como en un centro de formación e investigación. En la actualidad, un arboreto, una colección de orquídeas, jardines de rocas y de exposición, se encuentran entre los jardines más interesantes así como un enorme invernadero.

L'allestimento della tenuta di Wisley, di 97 ettari, è da ricondurre a un "Oakwood experimental garden", realizzato nel 1878 da George Ferguson Wilson con l'intento di coltivare con successo piante difficili. Nel 1903 la Royal Horticultural Society fece di Wisley uno dei più bei parchi dell'Inghilterra meridionale, eleggendolo anche a sede di un centro di formazione e di ricerca. Oggi anche un arboreto, una collezione di orchidee, giardini giapponesi, giardini espositivi e la vastissima serra offrono spunti.

The Glasshouse (right), opened in 2007, is equal in size to ten tennis courts and has different climatic zones creating habitats for plants from all around the world.

Das 2007 eröffnete Gewächshaus (rechts) ist so groß wie zehn Tennisplätze und zeigt Pflanzen aus aller Welt in unterschiedlichen Habitaten.

La serre (à droite), inaugurée en 2007, aussi grande que dix courts de tennis, comprend différentes zones climatiques assurant aux plantes du monde entier des conditions d'habitat idéales.

El invernadero (derecha), inaugurado en 2007, ocupa la superficie de diez canchas de tenis, e incluye diferentes zonas climáticas que dan cobijo a plantas de todo el mundo.

La serra (a destra), inaugurata nel 2007, ha le dimensioni di dieci campi da tennis e contiene piante di ogni parte del mondo in habitat differenti.

Eleven trial gardens feature plant collections for amateur gardeners to cultivate—with easy-care or traditional horticultural methods and intensive gardening.

Elf Mustergärten mit Bepflanzungen von pflegeleicht über familiengerecht bis hin zu extrem pflegebedürftig regen zum Nachahmen an.

Onze jardins didactiques présentent aux amateurs une palette de plantes à cultiver – plantes peu exigeantes ou pour la culture familiale ou demandant des soins intensifs.

Once jardines de exposición con especies que van desde el fácil cuidado, a las que se cultivan según los métodos horticulturales tradicionales y hasta las más delicadas y complejas.

Undici giardini espositivi con piante di facile coltivazione, piante adatte a famiglie e piante estremamente delicate offrono un'infinità di spunti.

RHS Rosemoor Gardens

Great Torrington, Devon, England

RHS Garden Rosemoor was donated to the Royal Horticultural Society by Lady Anne Berry in 1988, and has since been developed into 65 acres of beautiful garden and woodland, all reflecting the history of the site and the characteristic style of many West Country gardens. Today, visitors can relax at Lady Anne's original garden, take a leisurely stroll around the beautiful stream and lake, gain fantastic ideas from the fruit and vegetable garden or wander through the stylish formal gardens.

RHS Garden Rosemoor wurde 1988 der Royal Horticultural Society durch Lady Anne Berry gestiftet und seitdem zu einem 26 Hektar großen herrlichen Garten und Waldgebiet erweitert, welche die Geschichte des Ortes und den charakteristischen Stil vieler Gärten Südwestenglands widerspiegeln. Besucher können heute im einst von Lady Anne angelegten Garten entspannen, einen gemächlichen Spaziergang entlang dem schönen Fluss und See genießen, fantastische Ideen im Obst- und Gemüsegarten erhalten oder durch die formalen Gärten wandern.

En 1988, Lady Anne Berry fit don de RHS Garden Rosemoor à la Royal Horticultural Society qui en a fait depuis un domaine de 26 hectares de merveilleux jardins et zones boisées qui reflète l'histoire du lieu et le style caractéristique de nombreux jardins du sud-ouest de l'Angleterre. Aujourd'hui, les visiteurs peuvent se détendre dans les jardins aménagés jadis par Lady Anne, marcher tranquillement au bord de la jolie rivière et du lac, rassembler des idées fantastiques dans le potager et le verger et se promener dans les jardins soigneusement dessinés.

El jardín de RHS Rosemoor fue donado a la Royal Horticultural Society por Lady Anne Berry, y desde entonces ha ido convirtiéndose en 26 hectáreas de magníficos jardines y bosques que reflejan la historia local y el estilo característico de numerosos jardines del suroeste de Inglaterra. Actualmente los visitantes pueden relajarse en los jardines diseñados por Lady Anne, disfrutar dando un paseo a orillas del río y el lago, dejarse inspirar por los jardines de frutas y hortalizas o recorrer tranquilamente los jardines formales.

RHS Garden Rosemoor fu donato nel 1988 alla Royal Horticultural Society da Lady Anne Berry, e man mano ampliato fino a divenire uno splendido giardino e un bosco di 26 ettari, che rispecchiano la storia del luogo e lo stile caratteristico di molti parchi dell'Inghilterra meridionale. Oggi i visitatori possono rilassarsi nel giardino un tempo allestito da Lady Anne, fare una tranquilla passeggiata lungo il fiume e il lago, lasciarsi ispirare dalle idee fornite dal frutteto e dall'orto o visitare i giardini formali.

The famous rose gardens have more than 2,000 roses (200 varieties).

Die berühmten Rosengärten präsentieren über 2.000 Rosen in 200 verschiedenen Sorten.

Les célèbres roseraies ont plus de 2000 roses représentant 200 espèces.

Los famosos jardines de rosas tienen más de 2.000 rosas de 200 variedades diferentes.

I famosi roseti hanno più di 2.000 rose di 200 specie differenti.

166   RHS Rosemoor Gardens *Great Torrington, Devon, England*

RHS Rosemoor Gardens *Great Torrington, Devon, England* 167

Rosemoor's formal gardens have a number of stone features nestled within flowerbeds.

Rosemoors formale Gärten zeigen einige Skulpturen aus Stein, die in Blumenbeete eingebettet sind.

Les jardins de Rosemoor de conception formelle sont agrémentés de quelques sculptures de pierre placées au sein des massifs de fleurs.

Los jardines formales de Rosemoor incluyen algunas esculturas pétreas insertadas en parterres florales.

Nei giardini formali di Rosemoor le sculture di pietra sono collocate in aiuole fiorite.

Sezincote House & Garden

near Moreton-in-Marsh, Gloucestershire, England

When Charles Cockerell, who lived for many years in Bengal, inherited Sezincote, he asked his brother Samuel (a respected architect) to assist him building a house in Indian Mogul style. The house is surrounded by a romantic garden with typical Indian water garden and reflecting pools, grottoes and a Hindu temple. The remainder of the estate, which is in more traditional English landscape garden style, repeatedly reveals Indian influences, such as the Temple of Surya, the Brahmin bulls on the bridge or snake at serpents pond.

Als Charles Cockerell, der zuvor lange in Bengalen gelebt hatte, Sezincote erbte, bat er seinen Bruder Samuel 1810, ihm ein Haus im Mogulstil zu bauen. Direkt an das Haus schließt sich ein romantischer Garten mit typisch indischen Wasserläufen, Bassins, Grotten und ein Hindutempel an. Auch im übrigen Gartenbereich, der wesentlich den Traditionen eines englischen Landschaftsgartens folgt, finden sich immer wieder indische Anklänge, etwa im Tempel des Gottes Surya, dem Schmuck der Brücke mit brahmanischen Stieren oder der Schlange am Schlangenteich.

Quand Charles Cockerell, qui vécut de longues années au Bengale, hérita de Sezincote, il pria son frère Samuel, en 1810, de lui construire une maison de style moghol. Un jardin romantique jouxte la maison, avec ses jardins d'eau typiquement indiens, ses bassins, ses grottes et un temple hindou. Le reste du domaine plutôt conçu dans la tradition paysagiste anglaise révèle de nombreuses influences indiennes telles que le Temple de Surya, les taureaux brahmanes sur le pont ou le serpent du lac aux serpents.

Charles Cockerell vivió durante muchos años en Bengala. Cuando en 1810 heredó Sezincote, pidió a su hermano Samuel que le ayudara a construir una casa al estilo mogol indio. La mansión está rodeada por un romántico jardín con típicos estanques y jardines acuáticos indios, grutas y un templo hindú. También en el resto de la zona ajardinada, que principalmente sigue la tradición de un jardín paisajista inglés, pueden encontrarse influencias indias, como el Templo de Surya, los toros brahmánicos sobre el puente o la serpiente del estanque de las culebras.

Nel 1810 Charles Cockerell ereditò Sezincote. Egli aveva vissuto per lungo tempo nel Bengala; per questo motivo, incaricò il fratello Samuel di farvi costruire una casa in stile mogul, circondata da un romantico giardino di gusto tipicamente indiano, con corsi d'acqua, stagni, grotte e un tempio indù. Anche le altre aree, che seguono essenzialmente la tradizione del giardino all'inglese, contengono elementi di ispirazione indiana, come il tempio di Surya, i tori di Brahma sul ponte o il serpente presso l'omonimo stagno.

Sezincote's extensive, semi-circular winter garden, enclosed by the house and a hexagonal pavilion, is reminiscent of an orangery.

Der riesige halbrunde Wintergarten Sezincotes, begrenzt vom Haus und einem sechseckigen Pavillon, erinnert an eine Orangerie.

L'immense jardin d'hiver demi-circulaire de Sezincote, flanqué de la maison et d'un pavillon hexagonal, ressemble à une orangerie.

El enorme jardín de invierno semicircular de Sezincotes, limitado por la casa y un pabellón hexagonal, recuerda a un invernáculo.

Il vastissimo giardino d'inverno semicircolare di Sezincote, delimitato dalla casa e da un padiglione esagonale, ricorda un'orangerie.

172   Sezincote House & Garden *near Moreton-in-Marsh, Gloucesterhire, England*

The distant *view of the oriental dome of the pavilion from various parts of this English landscape garden recalls the creators' love of India.*

In einigen *Teilen des englischen Landschaftsgartens erinnert nur der ferne Anblick der orientalischen Kuppel an die Indienliebe der Erbauer.*

Apercevoir au *loin, dans certaines parties de ce jardin paysager anglais, la coupole orientale du pavillon rappelle combien son créateur aimait l'Inde.*

En algunos *lugares del jardín paisajista inglés se perfila, a lo lejos, la cúpula oriental que realza la gran pasión india de su creador.*

In alcune *parti del giardino all'inglese, la vista della lontana cupola orientale ricorda l'amore del costruttore per l'India.*

Sissinghurst Castle
Sissinghurst, Cranbrook, Kent, England

Sissinghurst Castle Garden is among the most celebrated gardens in the world. Amid the ruin of an old, Elizabethan castle, in the 1930s the writer, Vita Sackville-West and her husband and diplomat, Sir Harold Nicolson, designed ten enclosed garden compartments that follow a theme. Each of the separate gardens is distinguished by perfectly clipped yew hedges and bordered by walls of the old outbuildings. The Front Courtyard with its famous purple border, lower courtyard, spectacular White Garden, Rose Garden, Lime Walk with colourful spring flowerbeds and Cottage Garden are all developed here.

Die Gartenanlage von Sissinghurst gehört zu den populärsten der Welt. Zwischen den Ruinen eines alten elisabethanischen Schlosses gestalteten die Dichterin Vita Sackville-West und ihr Ehemann, der Diplomat Sir Harold Nicolson, in den 1930er-Jahren zehn abgeschlossene Gartenräume, die alle einem Thema folgen. Untergliedert durch akkurat geschnittene Eibenhecken und Mauern ehemaliger Gebäude wurden hier der Obere Hof mit seiner berühmten violetten Rabatte, der Untere Hof, der spektakuläre Weiße Garten, der Rosengarten, der Lindengang mit farbenfrohen Frühjahrsbeeten und der Bauerngarten angelegt.

Les jardins de Sissinghurst sont l'un des parcs les plus populaires au monde. Parmi les ruines d'un ancien château élisabéthain, la poétesse Vita Sackville-West et son mari, le diplomate Sir Harold Nicolson, aménagèrent dans les années 1930 une dizaine de clos à thèmes. Chaque espace est délimité par des haies d'ifs soigneusement taillés et les murs des anciennes dépendances. Ainsi sont mis en scène la cour supérieure avec son célèbre parterre pourpre, la cour basse, le magnifique jardin blanc, la roseraie, l'allée des tilleuls bordée de plates-bandes multicolores et le jardin du cottage.

Los jardines del castillo de Sissinghurst son famosos en el mundo entero. En la década de los 30 del siglo XX, entre las ruinas de un antiguo castillo isabelino, la poetisa Vita Sackville-West y su esposo, el diplomático Sir Harold Nicolson, diseñaron diez espacios ajardinados cerrados con un tema cada uno. Diferenciados perfectamente por setos de tejo y los muros del antiguo edificio, se crearon el patio superior, con sus famosos arriates violetas, el patio inferior, el espectacular jardín blanco, el jardín de rosas, el paseo de tilos con coloridos parterres de flores primaverales y el huerto de ocio.

Il giardino di Sissinghurst è tra i più popolari del mondo. Tra le rovine di un antico castello vittoriano, la poetessa Vita Sackville-West e il marito, il diplomatico Sir Harold Nicolson, allestirono negli anni trenta dieci giardini chiusi sulla base di un unico tema. Divisi da siepi di tassi accuratamente potate e dalle mura di edifici preesistenti, si possono ammirare il cortile superiore con la celebre aiuola viola, il cortile inferiore, lo spettacolare giardino bianco, il roseto, la passeggiata dei tigli con variopinte aiuole primaverili e l'orto.

Literature and nature in harmony: Vita Sackville-West wanted her garden to revive the atmosphere of her childhood.

Literatur im Einklang mit der Natur: Vita Sackville-West ließ in diesem Garten das Lebensgefühl ihrer Kindheit wieder aufleben.

Littérature et nature en harmonie : Vita Sackville-West désirait que revive dans son jardin l'atmosphère de son enfance.

Literatura y naturaleza en armonía: Vita Sackville-West deseaba que su jardín reflejara el ambiente de su niñez.

Letteratura e natura in armonia: con il suo giardino, Vita Sackville-West ha voluto rievocare l'atmosfera della sua infanzia.

Sissinghurst Castle *Sissinghurst, Cranbrook, Kent, England*   181

The White Garden (above right) is the most famous section—only white-flowering plants are grown or those with silvery-white foliage.

Der berühmteste Bereich ist der Weiße Garten (oben rechts), in dem ausschließlich weiß blühende Pflanzen oder solche mit silbrig-weißen Blättern gepflanzt sind.

Le jardin blanc (en haut à droite), la partie la plus connue, est planté exclusivement d'espèces à floraison blanche ou au feuillage blanc argenté.

El jardín blanco (arriba a la derecha) es el área más famosa; en ella, florecen exclusivamente flores blancas o plantas de hojas blancas y plateadas.

La sezione più conosciuta è il giardino bianco (in alto a destra), in cui vengono coltivate esclusivamente piante dai fiori bianchi o dalle foglie bianco-argentee.

182   Sissinghurst Castle   *Sissinghurst, Cranbrook, Kent, England*

Stourhead

near Stourton, Wiltshire, England

Stourhead is considered one of the earliest and finest examples of 18th century English landscape gardening. The mansion house is situated amid gardens, which are inspired by idealized 17th century Italian and French landscape paintings, and numerous classical features from architectural garden design: temples, grottoes, reflecting pools, the Palladian bridge and Pantheon. Meandering walkways, stunning viewpoints and picturesque vistas create harmony within a garden where nothing is left to chance. Stourhead was thus created as an antique arcadia.

Stourhead gilt als einer der frühsten und schönsten englischen Landschaftsgärten des 18. Jahrhunderts. An das Herrenhaus schließt sich eine von Ideallandschaften der italienischen und französischen Malerei des 17. Jahrhunderts inspirierte Gartenanlage mit zahlreichen klassizistischen Gartenarchitekturen an — Tempeln, Grotten, Wasserbecken, der Brücke im Palladio-Stil und dem Pantheon. Durch ein System von verschlungenen Wegen, Blickachsen und pittoresken Bildern verbunden, das nichts dem Zufall überlässt, entstand so ein antikes Arkadien.

Stourhead est considéré comme l'un des premiers et des plus beaux exemples de jardin paysager anglais du 18ème siècle. Autour du manoir s'étend un parc inspiré des paysages idéalisés dans les peintures italiennes et françaises du 17ème siècle et agrémenté de nombreux ornements architecturaux classiques: temple, grotte, bassin, le pont palladien et le panthéon. Par une subtile succession de chemins tortueux, de perspectives et de tableaux pittoresques qui ne doit rien au hasard, Stourhead apparaît comme une Arcadie antique.

Stourhead está considerado como uno de los jardines más antiguos y bellos del paisajismo inglés del siglo XVIII. La mansión se encuentra rodeada de jardines inspirados en la pintura paisajística italiana y francesa del siglo XVII, con numerosos edificios arquitecturales paisajísticos: templos, grutas, estanques, el puente palladiano y el panteón. Una serie de senderos entrelazados, miradores impresionantes y vistas pintorescas en los que nada es fruto de la casualidad, dieron lugar a esta antigua arcadia.

Stourhead è uno dei giardini all'inglese più antichi e belli del XVIII secolo. Intorno alla dimora si apre un parco ispirato ai paesaggi ideali della pittura italiana e francese del XVII secolo, con numerosi esempi di architettura da giardino di stampo classicistico: tempietti, grotte, specchi d'acqua, il ponte palladiano e il Pantheon. Grazie ad un sistema fatto di sentieri intrecciati, assi visuali e scorci pittoreschi che nulla lascia al caso, a Stourhead sembra rivivere un'antica Arcadia.

*The **Palladian** mansion house is the second of its kind in England.*

*Das **Herrenhaus** wurde im Stile Palladios erbaut und ist das zweite seiner Art in England.*

*Le **manoir** palladien est le deuxième de ce type en Angleterre.*

*La **mansión** de estilo palladiano es la segunda de su clase en Inglaterra.*

*La **dimora** in stile palladiano, la seconda di questo tipo esistente in Inghilterra.*

188   Stourhead *near Stourton, Wiltshire, England*

The River *Stour was dammed to create a great lake, forming the centre of the garden. Beautiful vistas and pathways are interconnected with this central point as the inspiration for the garden's location.*

Die Anstauung *des Flüsschens Stour zum See, der das Zentrum des Gartens bildet und auf den die Blick- und Wegachsen bezogen sind, war der Auftakt zur Anlage des Gartens.*

La rivière *Stour, endiguée pour créer un lac qui se trouve au centre du parc et vers lequel convergent les chemins et les perspectives, fut déterminante dans l'élaboration du jardin.*

El riachuelo *Stour fue convertido en el estanque que constituye el centro del jardín. Las bellas vistas y los senderos están interconectados con el punto central, que inspira al jardín en su conjunto.*

Il lago *formato dal fiumicello Stour, che costituisce il centro del giardino e a cui fanno riferimento l'asse visuale e l'asse di spostamento, è stato il punto di partenza per la realizzazione del giardino.*

190   Stourhead *near Stourton, Wiltshire, England*

The Lost Gardens of Heligan

St. Austell, Cornwall, England

Heligan was the seat of the Tremayne family for over 400 years. The garden's heyday was in the late 19th century. However, at the outbreak of the First World War the estate fell into neglect and was lost. Since 1990, the garden has been restored. The estate has award-winning features, historic buildings, romantic ornamental gardens with historical plants from all over the world, a subtropical jungle and a pioneering wildlife project, where flora and fauna can be observed in the wild landscape.

Heligan war mehr als 400 Jahre lang Wohnsitz der Familie Tremayne. Der Garten erlebte Ende des 19. Jahrhunderts seine Blüte. Mit Ausbruch des Ersten Weltkriegs geriet er jedoch in Vergessenheit und verfiel. Ab 1990 wurde der Garten restauriert. Das Anwesen zeigt preisgekrönte Besonderheiten, historische Gebäude, romantische Ziergärten mit historischen Pflanzen aus aller Welt, einen subtropischen Dschungel und ein wegweisendes Tierschutzprojekt, bei dem eine nahezu naturbelassene Landschaft und das dortige Tierleben beobachtet werden können.

Heligan fut la résidence de la famille Tremayne pendant plus de 400 ans. Le jardin connut son âge d'or à la fin du 19ème siècle. Mais quand éclata la première guerre mondiale, le domaine tomba dans l'oubli et le délabrement. Il fut restauré à partir de 1990. Le domaine possède des particularités qui ont remporté de nombreux prix, des bâtiments historiques, des jardins d'ornement romantiques plantés d'espèces historiques du monde entier, une jungle subtropicale et un projet pionnier de protection des animaux grâce auquel on peut admirer la flore et la faune dans un paysage pratiquement naturel.

Heligan fue la residencia de la familia Tremayne durante más de 400 años. El jardín vivió su máximo esplendor a finales del siglo XIX. Sin embargo, con el comienzo de la Primera Guerra Mundial, cayó en el olvido y se perdió. Desde 1990, el jardín se ha ido restaurando. La propiedad incluye singularidades premiadas, edificios históricos, románticos jardines de recreo con plantas históricas procedentes de todo el mundo, una selva subtropical, así como un proyecto pionero de protección de animales en el que la flora y fauna pueden observarse en el paisaje silvestre.

Heligan è stata per più di 400 anni la residenza della famiglia Tremayne. Il giardino ha raggiunto il culmine dello splendore alla fine del XIX secolo. Con lo scoppio della prima guerra mondiale, tuttavia, cadde in abbandono. Dopo il 1990 fu restaurato. La tenuta ha attrazioni notevolissime: romantici giardini con piante storiche originarie di ogni parte del mondo, una giungla subtropicale e un progetto di protezione della fauna, che permette di osservare il paesaggio quasi intatto e la fauna locale.

Even fairly eccentric design ideas such as "Giants Head" (far left) or "Mud Maid" (p. 194 / 195) find their place here.

Auch ziemlich „verrückte" Gestaltungsideen wie „Giants Head" (ganz links) oder die „Mud Maid" (S. 194 / 195) haben hier ihren Platz.

On rencontre ici des idées d'aménagement assez « excentriques », telles que ces « Giants Head » (tout à gauche) ou « Mud Maid » (p. 194 / 195).

Incluso algunos diseños excéntricos como "Giants Head" (izquierda extrema) o "Mud Maid" (pág. 194 / 195) encuentran su lugar.

Qui trovano posto anche idee stravaganti, come "Giants Head" (a sinistra) o "Mud Maid" (pag. 194 / 195).

Thanks to the region's microclimate, the jungle with subtropical plants flourishes with a profusion of tree ferns, giant rhubarb and banana palms, giving the impression that this area was established over many centuries.

Dank des Mikroklimas gedeiht der Dschungel mit subtropischen Pflanzen wie Baumfarne, Riesenrhabarber und Bananenpalmen üppig und mutet an, als sei er über Jahrtausende gewachsen.

Grâce au microclimat de la région, une jungle avec des plantes subtropicales prospère dans une profusion de fougères arborescentes, de rhubarbe géante et de palmiers, donnant l'impression d'occuper le terrain depuis des siècles.

Gracias al microclima de la región, la selva con plantas subtropicales florece con una profusión de helechos arborescentes, ruibarbos gigantes y plataneros que dan la impresión de haber sido plantados siglos atrás.

Grazie al microclima, la giungla con piante subtropicali come felci, rabarbari giganti e palme da banana prospera come se fosse cresciuta nel corso dei millenni.

Trebah Gardens
Falmouth, Cornwall, England

Trebah is Celtic for "The House on the Bay". A narrow inlet leads into this bay, shaped by a small meandering stream, where Charles Fox created a charming garden with many subtropical plants from around the world. Thanks to the mild Gulf Stream climate the plants magnificently flourished: giant ferns, palms, bamboo, rhododendrons and many others. After 40 years, when the gardens at Trebah fell into decay, the current owners restored the estate to make these gardens once again one of Cornwall's most beautiful garden locations.

Der Name Trebah steht im Keltischen für „Haus an der Bucht". Zu dieser Bucht führt eine schmale Schlucht, die ein kleiner Wasserlauf durchzieht und in der Charles Fox einen reizvollen Garten mit vielen subtropischen Gewächsen aus aller Welt schuf. Dank des milden Golfstromklimas gedieh alles prächtig: Riesenfarne, Palmen, Bambus, Rhododendren und vieles mehr. Nachdem Trebah über 40 Jahre lang verwilderte, haben ihn die heutigen Besitzer wieder zu einem der schönsten Gärten in ganz Cornwall gemacht.

En celtique, Trebah signifie « maison dans la baie ». Un ravin abrupt traversé par un petit ruisseau débouche sur cette baie – c'est là que Charles Fox créa un jardin enchanteur avec une multitude de plantes subtropicales du monde entier. Grâce à la douceur du climat due au gulf stream, fougères géantes, palmiers, bambous, rhododendrons, et bien d'autres plantes prospèrent merveilleusement. Laissé à l'abandon pendant 40 ans, Trebah est redevenu, après une restauration menée à bien par ses actuels propriétaires, l'un des plus beaux jardins de Cournouailles.

Trebah significa "Casa a orillas de la bahía" en el lenguaje celta córnico. Una estrecha garganta conduce a esta bahía, por la que fluye una pequeña corriente, donde Charles Fox creó un encantador jardín con numerosas plantas subtropicales de todo el mundo. Gracias al suave clima de la corriente del golfo, todo florece con exuberancia: helechos gigantes, palmeras, bambús, rododendros y mucho más. Tras más de 40 años en los que Trebah crecía salvaje, los actuales propietarios han restaurado el jardín para convertirlo de nuevo en uno de los más bellos de Cornualles.

Il nome celtico Trebah significa "Casa sulla baia". A questa baia conduce una stretta gola in cui scorre un piccolo corso d'acqua e in cui Charles Fox ha realizzato un delizioso giardino che accoglie piante subtropicali di tutto il mondo. Grazie al clima mite della corrente del Golfo, la vegetazione è rigogliosissima: felci giganti, palme, bambù, rododendri e molte altre specie. Dopo essere caduta in abbandono per 40 anni, Trebah è tornato ad essere uno dei più bei parchi di tutta la Cornovaglia grazie all'impegno che gli attuali proprietari gli hanno dedicato.

*A **"Bamboo Trail"** and lake are a part of Trebah's scenery as well as 2.5 acres filled with hydrangeas.*

*Ein **Bambuspfad** und ein See gehören ebenso zur Kulisse in Trebah wie ein ganzer Hektar voller Hortensien.*

*Un « **sentier de bambous** », un lac ainsi qu'un hectare entier d'hortensias font partie du décor à Trebah.*

*Una **"senda de bambú"** y un estanque son parte del magnífico escenario que brinda Trebah, al igual que su hectárea de hortensias.*

*Un **"sentiero di bambù"**, un lago e un intero ettaro ricoperto di ortensie fanno parte dello scenario di Trebah.*

The "Beach Path" leads through a mass of many exotic plants directly to the beach at Helford River estuary.

Der „Beach Path" führt durch eine Fülle vielfältiger exotischer Gewächse direkt zum Strand der Mündung des Helford-Flusses.

Le chemin de la plage passe au milieu d'une multitude de plantes exotiques et rejoint l'embouchure de la rivière Helford et la plage.

El sendero "Beach Path" nos conduce por una gran variedad de plantas exóticas hasta la playa de la desembocadura del río Helford.

Attraverso un'infinità di piante esotiche di ogni genere, il "Beach Path" conduce direttamente alla spiaggia alla foce del fiume Helford.

Trentham Estate

Trentham, Staffordshire, England

Trentham Estate is so impressive that over the centuries the great garden designers seem to have joined forces to ensure its creation. Sir Charles Barry originally designed the garden in about 1850 for the Duke of Sutherland. Since 2004, a restoration project has breathed new life into this vast park with an Italian Garden, Upper Flower Garden, pleasure garden on the western side with small show gardens, maze and Barefoot Walk as well as natural planting with 'Rivers of Grass' and a 'Floral Labyrinth' on the garden's eastern side.

Trentham Estate wirkt, als hätten große Gartendesigner über die Jahrhunderte hinweg Hand in Hand gearbeitet. Ursprünglich entwarf Sir Charles Barry um 1850 den Garten für den Herzog von Sutherland. Ab 2004 wurde der riesige Garten sehr aufwendig restauriert. Jetzt gibt es in dieser vielseitigen Anlage den Italienischen Garten, den oberen Blumengarten, den westlichen Lustgarten mit kleinen Schaugärten, Strauchlandschaften und Barfußpfad sowie den östlichen Lustgarten, der sich durch seine sehr natürlich wirkende Grasbepflanzung und ein Pflanzenlabyrinth auszeichnet.

À Trentham Estate, on dirait que de grands créateurs de jardin ont uni leurs talents pendant des siècles. Sir Charles Barry dessina ce jardin vers 1850 pour le Duc de Sutherland. En 2004, un vaste projet de restauration redonna vie à cet immense parc où il y a un jardin à l'italienne, un jardin de fleurs en hauteur, un jardin de plaisir côté ouest avec de petits jardins d'exposition, des arbustes et un sentier aux pieds nus et, côté est, une plantation quasi naturelle d'herbes ornementales et un labyrinthe de verdure.

Trentham Estate es tan impresionante que parece que los grandes paisajistas hubieran unido sus fuerzas para crear esta joya. Sir Charles Barry diseñó el jardín original, alrededor del año 1850, para el duque de Sutherland. Desde 2004, el enorme jardín ha dado nueva vida a este gran lugar. Ahora incluye un jardín italiano, el jardín de flores superior, el jardín de recreo occidental con pequeños jardines de exhibición, paisajes de arbustos y un sendero para caminar descalzo, así como el jardín de recreo oriental, caracterizado por su césped de aspecto altamente natural y un laberinto vegetal.

Trentham Estate appare come un luogo in cui grandi architetti abbiano lavorato in stretta collaborazione nel corso dei secoli. Fu Sir Charles Barry, intorno al 1850, a progettare questo giardino per il duca di Sutherland. Dopo il 2004, il vastissimo parco venne restaurato con molta cura. Oggi questa multiforme tenuta accoglie il giardino italiano, il giardino fiorito superiore, il giardino delle delizie occidentale con piccoli giardini espositivi, arbusti e un sentiero da percorrere a piedi scalzi, nonché il giardino delle delizie orientale, coltivato a prato, con un labirinto di piante.

Designed by *Piet Oudolf: the Floral Labyrinth (left), Rivers of Grass (p. 206 top) and two, 394-ft long flowering borders (p. 207).*

Von Piet *Oudolf gestaltet: Das Pflanzenlabyrinth (links), die Graslandschaft (S. 206 oben) und zwei, je 120 m lange Blumenrabatten (S. 207).*

Aménagé par *Piet Oudolf: le labyrinthe de verdure (à gauche), la plantation d'herbes ornementales (p. 206 en haut) et deux plates-bandes de fleurs de 120 m de long (p. 207).*

Diseñado por *Piet Oudolf: el laberinto floral (izquierda), el paisaje de hierba (pág. 206 arriba) y dos arriates de flores de 120 m de longitud cada uno (pág. 207).*

Il labirinto *di piante (a sinistra), la prateria (pag. 206 in alto) e due aiuole fiorite di 120 m ciascuna (pag. 207) sono stati realizzati da Piet Oudolf.*

To this day, the Italian Garden is preserved in Charles Barry's original design—an enchanting sight at any time of the day and season.

Der Italienische Garten hat sich in der Gestaltung von Charles Barry bis heute erhalten und verzaubert zu jeder Tages- und Jahreszeit.

Le jardin à l'italienne dessiné par Charles Barry a été conservé jusqu'à aujourd'hui et enchante les visiteurs à toute heure du jour et en toutes saisons.

El jardín italiano ha mantenido su diseño de Charles Barry hasta hoy, y engatusa a cualquier hora y día del año.

Il giardino italiano è stato mantenuto fino ad oggi nell'allestimento di Charles Barry ed è incantevole ad ogni ora del giorno ed in qualsiasi stagione.

Veddw House

Devauden, Monmouthshire, Wales

Veddw House Garden earns high praise from all circles for its exquisite proportions, its creation of harmony between house, garden and surrounding landscape, its perfect blend of wilderness and formal parterre and, last but not least, its charisma. Veddw House is less about an exceptional collection of plants than an overall idea and dramatic effect: the combination of colours and forms is supremely successful. Its reflecting pool, borders overflowing with grasses and wave-like hedges are particularly stunning.

Hohes Lob von vielen Seiten bekommt der Veddw House Garten für seine exzellente Proportionierung, seine zwischen Haus, Garten und Umgebung bestehende Harmonie, seine gelungene Mischung aus Wildnis und formaler Anlage sowie für seine Ausstrahlung. Veddw House steht weniger für spezielle Pflanzen als für den Gesamteffekt, die außergewöhnlich gelungene Kombinationswirkung aus Farben und Formen. Besonders spektakulär sind der die Umgebung reflektierende Pool, die Grasbeete und die zu Wellen geschnittenen Hecken.

Les éloges sur Veddw House Garden sont unanimes : pour l'excellence des proportions, l'harmonie régnant entre la maison, le jardin et l'environnement, le juste mélange de paysage sauvage et d'arrangement formel et surtout pour son rayonnement. Veddw House est moins réputé pour ses collections de plantes que pour l'atmosphère qu'il dégage, la combinaison extraordinairement réussie des couleurs et des formes. Les reflets dans l'eau du bassin, les plates-bandes d'herbacées et les vagues de haies taillées créent un effet spectaculaire.

El jardín de Veddw House cosecha grandes elogios de todo el mundo por sus exquisitas proporciones, su armonía entre casa, jardín y entorno, su lograda combinación de naturaleza silvestre y parterre formal, así como por su gran carisma. Veddw House no destaca tanto por sus plantas especiales como por su modo general y extraordinario de combinar formas y colores. Su piscina reflectante, los parterres de hierba y los setos cortados en forma de onda resultan especialmente espectaculares.

Veddw House Garten è apprezzato per le sue proporzioni perfette, per l'armonia tra casa, giardino e ambiente, per la riuscita combinazione tra natura selvaggia e allestimento formale, nonché per il suo fascino, originato non tanto da piante straordinarie quanto dall'effetto complessivo che colori e forme indovinati riescono a creare. La piscina che riflette l'ambiente circostante, le aiuole e le siepi ondulate sono uno spettacolo unico.

A familiar sight in the garden: thistles alongside roses (far left). View through Hornbeam Tunnel (right).

Ein häufiges Bild im Garten: Cardys neben Rosen (links außen). Ein Blick durch den Tunnel aus Hainbuchen (rechts).

Un tableau familier dans le jardin: des chardons à côté de roses (tout à gauche). Vue à travers la charmille (à droite).

Una vista familiar en el jardín: cardos junto a rosas (izquierda extrema). Vista por el túnel de carpes (derecha).

Cardi e rose (immagine esterna a sinistra) sono un accostamento frequente nel giardino. Veduta attraverso la galleria di carpini bianchi (a destra).

Memorial stones set into the flowerbeds are a reminder of forgotten local place names (below left).

In die Beete eingebettete Gedenksteine erinnern an vergessene Flurnamen (unten links).

Des pierres commémoratives logées dans des parterres de fleurs rappellent des lieux-dits oubliés (en bas à gauche).

Las piedras conmemorativas colocadas en los parterres recuerdan nombres locales olvidados (abajo a la izquierda).

Le lapidi nelle aiuole ricordano nomi locali dimenticati (in basso a sinistra).

Index

Adare, Limerick

Adare Manor

Garden designer: P. C. Hardwick

Garden location: Adare, Limerick, Ireland

Garden website: www.adaremanor.com

Northwich, Cheshire

Arley Hall & Gardens

Garden designer: Peter Warburton IV (18ᵗʰ century), William Emes under Sir Peter Warburton V, Rowland and Mary Egerton-Warburton (1846)

Garden location: Northwich, Cheshire, England, UK

Garden website: www.arleyhallandgardens.com

Bantry, Cork

Bantry House

Garden designer: Original garden plans in 1830s by Richard White, Second Earl of Bantry. Since 1997, restoration works continue under the current owners, Egerton and Brigitte Shelswell-Whit

Garden location: Bantry, Cork, Ireland

Garden website: www.bantryhouse.com

Barrington, Somerset

Barrington Court

Garden designer: Lyle family, inspired by Gertrude Jekyll (1917)

Garden location: Barrington, Somerset, England, UK

Garden website: www.nationaltrust.org.uk/main/w-vh/w-visits/w-findaplace/w-barringtoncourt/

Colchester, Essex

The Beth Chatto Gardens

Garden designer: Beth Chatto

Garden location: Colchester, Essex, England, UK

Garden website: www.bethchatto.co.uk

Tal-y-Cafn, Conwy

Bodnant

Garden designer: Created by the Aberconway family since 1875, today in fifth generation management

Garden location: Tal-y-Cafn, Conwy, Wales, UK

Garden website: www.bodnant-garden.co.uk

Buckfastleigh, Devon

Buckfast Abbey

Garden designer: The monks of Buckfast Abbey

Garden location: Buckfastleigh, Devon, England, UK

Garden website: www.buckfast.org.uk

Chirk, Wrexham

Chirk Castle

Garden designer: Formal pleasure garden: Sir Thomas Myddelton (1657); ironwork gates: Robert and John Davies (1709 to 1711); landscape garden: William Emes (1764); Norah Lindsay with Lord and Lady Howard de Walden (1911–1946)

Garden location: Chirk, Wrexham, Wales, UK

Garden website: www.chirk.com/castle.html
www.nationaltrust.org.uk/main/w-chirkcastle

Marldon, Paignton, Devon

Compton Castle

Garden designer: Gilbert family members

Garden location: Marldon, Paignton, Devon, England, UK

Garden website: www.nationaltrust.org.uk/main/w-comptoncastle

Banchory, Aberdeenshire

Crathes Castle

Garden designer: Sir James and Lady Sybil Burnett in the 1920s

Garden location: Banchory, Aberdeenshire, Scotland, UK

Garden website: www.nts.org.uk/Property/20/

Fontwell, West Sussex

Denmans Garden

Garden designer: Owned jointly by John Brookes MBE and Michael Neve

Garden location: Denmans Lane, Fontwell, West Sussex, England, UK

Garden website: www.denmans-garden.co.uk

Southampton, Hampshire

Exbury Gardens

Garden designer: Lionel Nathan de Rothschild (1919)

Garden location: Southampton, Hampshire, England, UK

Garden website: www.exbury.co.uk

Falkland, Fife

Falkland Palace

Garden designer: Percy Cane (1948)

Garden location: Falkland, Fife, Scotland, UK

Garden website: www.nts.org.uk/Property/93

Ockley, Surrey

Hannah Peschar Sculpture Garden

Garden designer: Hannah Peschar's husband, Anthony Paul (from the late 1970s)

Website: www.anthonypaullandscapedesign.com

Garden location: Ockley, Surrey, England, UK

Garden website: www.hannahpescharsculpture.com

Taunton, Somerset

Hestercombe Gardens

Garden designers: Landscape garden dating from the 1750s by Coplestone Warre Bampfylde. Restored since 1992 by Philip White; Victorian Terrace: first Viscount Portman (1873 to 1878); Edwardian Formal Garden: Sir Edwin Lutyens and Gertrude Jekyll (design 1903)

Garden location: Cheddon Fitzpaine, Taunton, Somerset, England, UK

Garden website: www.hestercombe.com

Poolewe, Highland

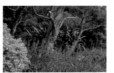

Inverewe Garden

Garden designer: Sir Osgood Mackenzie (1864), since 1922 his daughter Mairi Sawyer, and since 1952 The National Trust for Scotland

Garden location: Poolewe, Highland, Scotland, UK

Garden website: www.nts.org.uk/Property/36

Bodmin, Cornwall

Lanhydrock

Garden designer: George Truefitt (1857), crescent-shaped flowerbeds planted by Lady Clifden (1914), completed in 1971 by the National Trust. 7th Viscount Clifden (1930) added exceptional varieties of imported trees and shrubs

Garden location: Bodmin, Cornwall, England, UK

Garden website: www.nationaltrust.org.uk/main/w-lanhydrock

near Romsey, Hampshire

Mottisfont Abbey Garden

Garden designer: Gilbert and Maude Russell (from 1934); knot garden: Norah Lindsay (in the 1930s); north side of the house with lime avenue: Sir Geoffrey Jellicoe (from 1936); since 1972, under ownership of the National Trust. Rose garden (from 1972): Graham Stuart Thomas

Garden location: near Romsey, Hampshire, England, UK

Garden website: www.nationaltrust.org.uk/main/w-vh/w-visits/w-findaplace/w-mottisfont

East Cowes, Isle of Wight

Osborne House & Gardens

Garden designer: Thomas Cubitt and Prince Albert, terraces designed by Ludwig Gruner and Prince Albert, orchard restoration by Rupert Golby in 2000

Garden location: East Cowes, Isle of Wight, England, UK

Garden website: www.english-heritage.org.uk/server/show/nav.1082

Portmeirion, Gwynedd

Portmeirion

Garden designer: In the late 1850s, primarily Henry Seymour Westmacott, and later until about 1950, Caton Haigh with Alfred Blount. Formal gardens landscaped by Clough Williams-Ellis. Under the direction of Horticultural Director, Menna Angharad, the owners are completing a major renovation programme started by her mother Susan Williams-Ellis in 1980

Garden location: Portmeirion, Gwynedd, Wales, UK

Garden website: www.portmeirion-village.com

Welshpool, Powys

Powis Castle

Garden designer: William Winde under William Herbert, 1st Marquess of Powis

Garden location: Welshpool, Powys, Wales, UK

Garden website: www.nationaltrust.org.uk/main/w-powiscastle_garden

Woking, Surrey

RHS Garden Wisley

Garden designer: Small part of the garden's estate cultivated as "Oakwood experimental garden" by George Ferguson Wilson (1878); since 1903, developed by the Royal Horticultural Society

Garden location: Woking, Surrey, England, UK

Garden website: www.rhs.org.uk/whatson/gardens/wisley/index.asp

Great Torrington, Devon

RHS Rosemoor Gardens

Garden designer: Lady Anne Berry, (married surname, Palmer) and her mother from 1931. The Garden was gifted to the Royal Horticultural Society in 1988 and has since been developed into 65 acres

Garden location: Great Torrington, Devon, England, UK

Garden website: www.rhs.org.uk/rosemoor

near Moreton-in-Marsh, Gloucestershire

Sezincote House & Garden

Garden designer: Thomas Daniell and (probably) Humphry Repton, restored in the 1950s by Lady Kleinwort and Graham Stuart Thomas

Garden location: near Moreton-in-Marsh, Gloucestershire, England, UK

Garden website: www.sezincote.co.uk

Cranbrook, Kent

Sissinghurst Castle

Garden designer: Vita Sackville-West and her husband, Harold Nicolson (from 1930)

Garden location: Sissinghurst, Cranbrook, Kent, England, UK

Garden website: www.nationaltrust.org.uk/main/w-vh/w-visits/w-findaplace/w-sissinghurstcastlegarden

near Stourton, Wiltshire

Stourhead

Garden designer: Henry Hoare II in association with architect Henry Flitcroft (1741 to 1780), redesigned about 1800 by Hoare's heirs

Garden location: near Stourton, Wiltshire, England, UK

Garden website: www.nationaltrust.org.uk/main/w-stourhead

St. Austell, Cornwall

The Lost Gardens of Heligan

Garden designer: Original garden by Squire Henry Hawkins Tremayne (1766 to 1829) and Squire John Hearle Tremayne (1829 to 1851); today's garden was rediscovered in 1990 by Tim Smit and John Willis, a descendant of the Tremaynes. John Nelson, Philip McMillan Browse and local horticultural advisors restored and newly designed the garden to the original designs

Garden location: St. Austell, Cornwall, England, UK

Garden website: www.heligan.com

Falmouth, Cornwall

Trebah Gardens

Garden designer: Charles Fox (from 1840), Juliet and Edmund Backhouse (from 1876), Charles H. and Alice Hext (from 1907), restoration since 1980 by Major Tony Hibbert and his wife, Eira

Garden location: Falmouth, Cornwall, England, UK

Garden website: www.trebahgarden.co.uk

Trentham, Staffordshire

Trentham Estate

Garden designer: Original design by Sir Charles Barry, Capability Brown and Charles Bridgeman. New design by Tom Stuart-Smith (London, United Kingdom) and Piet Oudolf (Hummelo, The Netherlands)

Website: www.tomstuartsmith.co.uk, www.oudolf.com

Garden location: Trentham, Staffordshire, England, UK

Garden website: www.trentham.co.uk

Devauden, Monmouthshire

Veddw House

Garden designer: Anne Wareham and Charles Hawes

Garden location: Devauden, Monmouthshire, Wales, UK

Garden website: www.veddw.co.uk

Photo Credits

Aidan McRae Thomson	Sezincote House & Garden	170
Amy Wagner	Trebah Gardens	199
Anthony Smith	Barrington Court	33, 34 bottom
	Inverewe Garden	125, 126 top
	Powis Castle	155–157
	RHS Garden Wisley	158–163
Beryl Mc Millan	Stourhead	185
Brian Mottershead	Bodnant	back cover top left, 50, 51
Charles Hawes	Chirk Castle	61
	Veddw House	212–217
Chris Goddard	Barrington Court	32 right, 35, 37, 38
	Buckfast Abbey	54–59
	Compton Castle	68–75
	Lanhydrock	128, 130
	Osborne House & Gardens	142–147
	RHS Rosemoor Gardens	164–169
Clive Mollart and Trentham Estate	Trentham Estate	208 left
David Jennings	The Lost Gardens of Heligan	196 left
	Trebah Gardens	198 right
Dean Brindle	Portmeirion	148, 149, 151
Dianne Barton	Bodnant	53 top
Dr. Lok Raj	Bodnant	48–49, 53 bottom
Emma Fox and Trentham Estate	Trentham Estate	cover, 12, 204–207, 208 right–210
George Robins	Denmans Garden	86, 87 top left
	Mottisfont Abbey Garden	134 right, 135, 136 top, 140, 141 bottom
Hannah Peschar Sculpture Garden	Hannah Peschar Sculpture Garden	106–113
Helena Pugsley	Exbury Gardens	90 left, 91, 92, 93
	Mottisfont Abbey Garden	134 left, 136 bottom, 137–139, 141 top
Jane S. Young	Hestercombe Gardens	114–119
Janie Shelswell-White, John Hession, Bord Failte	Bantry House	27–30
Jean McCreanor	Bodnant	52
John Palmour	Sezincote House & Garden	173, 177 top
Julian Stephens, The Lost Gardens of Heligan	The Lost Gardens of Heligan	192–195, 197
Ken Hircock	Stourhead	back cover bottom right, 187, 190
Kevan Brewer, Exbury Gardens	Exbury Gardens	90 right, 92–95
Leslie Platt	Arley Hall	5, 20–25
	Bodnant	46 left
Lorna Tremayne, The Lost Gardens of Heligan	The Lost Gardens of Heligan	196 right
Marina Zschau	Sissinghurst	180 top, 182 left
Martin Snell	Denmans Garden	85, 86 bottom, 87 bottom, 88, 89
National Trust	Lanhydrock	129
NTS	Crathes Castle	76 right, 79
NTS, Brian and Nina Chapple	Crathes Castle	76 left, 77, 78, 82
	Inverewe Garden	120–124, 126 bottom, 127
NTS, Brian Chapple	Falkland Palace	104 bottom
	Inverewe Garden	124, 126 bottom
NTS, David Robertson	Falkland Palace	9, 98 right, 99, 105
	Inverewe Garden	120
NTS, Jim Henderson	Crathes Castle	80–81, 83
NTS, John Sinclair	Falkland Palace	100–103
NTS, Ken Whitcombe/ Kenbarry Photography	Falkland Palace	98 left
NTS, Mark Leman	Falkland Palace	104 top
Paul Chibeba	Denmans Garden	84, 87 top right
Paul Davis	Trebah Gardens	198 left, 200 top
Peter Ellison	Powis Castle	back cover top right, 153, 154
Ramon L. García González	Bantry House	26, 31
Richard Godwin	Chirk Castle	62, 63, 66, 67 top
Richard White	Sissinghurst	178, 180 bottom, 181, 182 right, 183
Rob Millenaar	Sissinghurst	179
Rob Roy	Portmeirion	150
Robert Williams	Bodnant	47
Roland Bauer	Adare Manor	back cover bottom left, 14–19
Courtesy	Sezincote House & Garden	7, 171, 172, 174, 176, 177 bottom
Stefan Pfaff	Chirk Castle	60 left, 65
Stella-Maria Thomas	Barrington Court	32 left, 34 top, 36, 39 bottom
Sue Craske	Chirk Castle	60 right, 64 left, 67 bottom
The Beth Chatto Gardens Ltd.	The Beth Chatto Gardens	40–45
Thomas Patterson	Bodnant	46 right
Trevor Lockyer	Barrington Court	39 top
	Stourhead	184, 186, 188, 189
Ute & Hans-Joachim Orth	Lanhydrock	131–133
	Trebah Gardens	200 bottom, 201–203
Wesley Kerr	Powis Castle	152

Produced by fusion publishing gmbh, berlin

Editorial team:

Elke Fleing (Editor & garden texts, introduction)

Katharina Feuer (Editorial coordination, Layout)

Sabine Scholz (Text coordination)

Dr. Suzanne Kirkbright, Artes Translations, UK (Translations)

Jan Hausberg, fusion publishing gmbh (Imaging & prepress)

Published by teNeues Publishing Group

teNeues Verlag GmbH & Co. KG
Am Selder 37, 47906 Kempen, Germany
Phone: 0049-(0)2152-916-0, Fax: 0049-(0)2152-916-111
E-mail: books@teneues.de

Press department: arehn@teneues.de
Phone: 0049-(0)2152-916-202

teNeues Publishing Company
16 West 22nd Street, New York, NY 10010, USA
Phone: 001-212-627-9090, Fax: 001-212-627-9511

teNeues Publishing UK Ltd.
York Villa, York Road, Byfleet, KT14 7HX, Great Britain
Phone: 0044-1932-4035-09, Fax: 0044-1932-4035-14

teNeues France S.A.R.L.
93, rue Bannier, 45000 Orléans, France
Phone: 0033-2-38541071, Fax: 0033-2-38625340

www.teneues.com

© 2009 teNeues Verlag GmbH + Co. KG, Kempen

ISBN: 978-3-8327-9300-5

Printed in Italy

Bibliographic information published by the Deutsche Nationalbibliothek. The Deutsche Nationalbibliothek lists this publication in the Deutsche Nationalbibliografie; detailed bibliographic data are available in the Internet at http://dnb.d-nb.de.